SHOES AND SHIPS AND SEALING WAX

An illustrated history of the Board of Trade 1786—1986

FRONTISPIECE: 'The President's Room', Board of Trade, by Thomas Rowlandson, 1809

DEPARTMENT OF TRADE AND INDUSTRY

Shoes and Ships and Sealing-Wax

An illustrated history of the Board of Trade 1786–1986

by Susan Foreman

LONDON : HER MAJESTY'S STATIONERY OFFICE

ISBN 0 11 513825 0

HMSO publications are available from:

HMSO Publications Centre
(Mail and telephone orders only)
PO Box 276, London SW8 5DT
Telephone order (01) 622 3316
General enquiries (01) 211 5656

HMSO Bookshops
49 High Holborn, London, WC1V 6HB (01) 211 5656 (Counter service only)
258 Broad Street, Birmingham, B1 2HE (021) 643 3757
Southey House, 33 Wine Street, Bristol, BS1 2BQ (0272) 24306/24307
9-21 Princess Street, Manchester, M60 8AS (061) 834 7201
80 Chichester Street, Belfast, ST1 4JY (0232) 234488
13a Castle Street, Edinburgh, EH2 3AR (031) 225 6333

HMSO's Accredited Agents
(see Yellow Pages)

And through good booksellers

Printed for Her Majesty's Stationery Office by BPCC Graphics, Derby
Dd. 738810 C40 10/85

Contents

1.
Headquarters
building, 1
Victoria Street,
London SW1.

Acknowledgements

I should like to thank the following people and organisations for their help and interest in this project: the Department of Trade and Industry Library Services for bearing the brunt of my demands, *British business*, the Curator of HM Coastguard Museum Brixham, Department of Energy Library, the Marine Library of the Department of Transport, the Public Record Office (source cited as BT), and HM Treasury Library Services.

Also, for their help over specific items I owe thanks to: Chris Murphy, Mary Lackey, Elizabeth Llewellyn Smith, the Lady Soames DBE, staff of Birmingham Reference Library, the Library of the House of Commons and the National Meteorological Library. The section on the European Communities was drafted by John Ingram and the final chapter by the Information Division of the Department of Trade and Industry.

Thanks are also due to the efficient and helpful staff of several museums and picture libraries, especially the BBC Hulton Picture Library, the Ironbridge Gorge Museum, the Mansell Collection, the Mary Evans Picture Library, the National Portrait Gallery, the Science Museum and V & A Museum, Westminster Public Library Archives, and my local public library at Rickmansworth, Hertfordshire. Last, but not least, that invaluable institution, the London Library.

Susan Foreman
Rickmansworth

October 1985

Picture Sources

Original illustrations collected by the author for this project, and cited as 'Author's collection' have been deposited in the DTI's Headquarters Library at 1 Victoria Street, London SW1. The numbers referred to are illustration numbers.

Associated Press: *117, 118, 151.*

Author's collection: *5, 7, 8, 11, 18, 23, 29, 32, 33, 76, 79, 81, 82, 92, 104, 108, 110, 137, 141, 170.*

Birmingham Public Libraries, Stone Collection: *69. 74.*

British Airways: *131.*

BBC Hulton Picture Library: *16, 36, 46, 54, 98, 113, 115, 119, 144, 150, 152.*

Central Office of Information: *40, 44, 70, 158.*

DTI Archives: *65.*

DTI Library: *2, 3, 4, 12, 14, 19, 20, 21, 24, 26, 50, 52, 53, 55, 56, 57, 60, 73, 75, 78, 90, 107* [flag], *128, 129, 132, 138, 139, 142, 146, 147, 156, 161, 164, 171, 173, 180, 181, 183.*

DTI Photographic Unit: *1, 13, 22, 58, 71, 93, 94, 127, 133, 134, 162,* inside back cover.

European Commission: *160.*

HM Coastguard Museum, Brixham; *120, 121, 122, 123, 124, 125.*

HM Treasury, Lister Collection: Inside front cover, *49, 72, 163, 175, 176, 177, 178,* back cover.

Illustrated London News: *77, 106.*

Trustees of the Imperial War Museum, London: *148, 149.*

Ironbridge Gorge Museum: *6, 31, 95.*

ITC Film Distributors: *84.*

Laboratory of the Government Chemist: *85.*

Lady Lee: *153.*

Elizabeth Llewellyn Smith: Frontispiece, *169.*

London School of Economics: *51.*

Mansell Collection: *25, 97, 99, 100, 135.*

Marine Library, Department of Transport: *101, 102, 105, 107* [handbill], *111, 112.*

Mary Evans Picture Library: *37, 38, 39, 41, 42, 43, 45, 48, 83, 96, 116, 140.*

National Engineering Laboratory: *86.*

National Meteorological Library: *103.*

National Physical Laboratory: *87, 88.*

National Portrait Gallery: *2, 9, 15, 167.*

National Portrait Gallery archive: *10, 91, 165, 166, 168.*

Patent Office: *59, 61, 62, 63, 64.*

Popperfoto: *47, 108, 126, 130, 143, 145, 155, 157.*

Press Association: *172.*

Public Record Office: *136.*

Reproduced by permission of *Punch*: *154.*

Royal Statistical Society: *17.*

Trustees of the Science Museum, London: *30, 67, 68.*

Scottish Office: *174.*

Reproduced by kind permission of Curtis Brown Ltd, London, on behalf of Lady Soames: *80*

Cartoon supplied by permission of *The Standard*: *66.*

Victoria and Albert Museum: Front cover.

Warren Spring Laboratory: *89.*

Westminster City Libraries, Archives department: *182.*

'THERE is probably no department of the Government to whose functions so many and such important additions have recently been made, as the Board of Trade. [But] its constitution has not yet been revised with a view to the efficient discharge of its new duties. Originally designed for consultative purposes, it was organised in a very different manner from the executive offices ... Of late years, however, a large amount of executive business, very important and very various in its nature, has been assigned to this Department. Thus in 1832 it was charged with the duty of collecting and publishing statistical information; since 1840 it has exercised a more or less minute control over the Railway companies; about the same time the Government School of Design was placed under its superintendence; the Office for the Registration of Designs, and that for the Registration of Joint Stock Companies, have also been attached to it; and within the last two years a new and most important addition has been made to its functions by the Acts for the Regulation of Merchant Shipping of the country, for the winding up and determination of the Merchant Seamen's Fund, and for the inspection of our steam navigation. As each of these subjects has been successively assigned to the Board of Trade, some provision has been made for supplying the machinery required to deal with it: but this has generally been done by adding to the Department either some new officer, or some subordinate Board ... and not by any such general recasting of the office as would render it efficient as a whole for the discharge of all its functions'.

From: *Northcote-Trevelyan report on civil service reform.* 1854.

Prologue

Throughout its long history the Board of Trade has encompassed such a wide range of interests that it has had a greater impact on the man

for many years had been closed to English trade, reopened pressure was put on the Council to deal with an increasing number of trade issues.

in the street than most government departments. Even now, sixteen years after its demise, the name 'Board of Trade' is in common parlance. Now translated into today's Department of Trade and Industry, the tradition continues and the wheel has come full circle from the 1786 Order in Council that established the Board of Trade 'for the consideration of all matters relating to trade'. But at different times in its history the Board has had a finger in almost every administrative pie, from the care of the colonies in the 18th and 19th centuries to clothes rationing in World War II, from regional policy to exporting, and from a suitable clerk's appointment as colonial bishop to the calibration of weights and measures.

The Board is, and always has been, a Committee of the Privy Council – that body of distinguished people who advise the Monarch. Before it was established, trade matters were dealt with by the Council itself. In Tudor times the Privy Council was much concerned with monopolies, the inadequacy of medieval methods of trade regulation, merchant companies and foreign trade. Trade problems were exacerbated by the Spanish wars and the fight for independence in the Low countries. When peace was made with Spain in 1604, and markets, which

The Committee of the Privy Council for Trade and Plantations was established in 1621 to relieve the Council of these tasks of dealing with merchants' complaints and of protecting England's overseas interests. King James I directed that the Committee should consider the 'true causes of the decay of trade and scarcity of coyne within this kingdom, and to consult of the meanes for removing of these inconveniences'. This instruction was reiterated in 1660 when *two* councils were appointed; one was to inspect and look after the plantations, the other (for trade) was to examine commercial treaties, regulate weights and measures, encourage fishing and coinage and develop the trade of the plantations. The Council of Trade was told 'Ye shall take into your consideration ye inconveniences [which] the English trade hath suffered in any parts beyond the seas. And are to enquire into such articles of former treaties as have been made with any princes or states in relation to trade'. The two councils were united in 1672 (by Patent) in a single standing council.

A permanent Committee was established by William III in 1696 with wider terms of reference and increased financial resources, and was called the Board of Trade and Plantations. This Board

I

was 'to examine into and take an account of the state and condition of the general trade of England and of the several particular trades into foreign parts ... to consider what means profitable manufactures already settled may be further improved and how other new and profitable manufactures may be introduced ...' The new body, like its predecessors, was intended to be advisory rather than administrative.

Among the duties of Committee members were the protection of merchant convoys against the Barbary pirates, an examination of the coral monopoly of Minorca, and a watch on the interests of the wool trade. The Committee was also responsible for looking after colonial settlers before they left Britain, and the provision of clergy, doctors and teachers when they arrived at their new home. Under its then president, Lord Halifax, it organised the colony of Nova Scotia whose capital is named after him.

Even in the early 18th century there were organised, if sporadic, attempts to collect commercial intelligence from overseas. In 1711 the Board ordered that a representation be prepared, proposing to Queen Anne that 'all the British consuls in foreign ports .. and her ministers there may ... every six months ... assemble the British merchants, trading in the place of such consul or minister's residence, and consult with them upon the then present state of British trade to that place and to propose what they think proper for the improvement or the advancement thereof ...' As a result the Board received reports from several commercial centres in 1712 and following years; it made no general attempt to obtain regular information on the state of trade until 1765. However, circular letters were sent intermittently to all consuls on particular problems. In 1728 the Board asked what duties were payable on any goods grown, produced or manufactured in Great

2. Edmund Burke.

Britain, in 1729 whether any new duties or hardships were laid on British trade, and in 1731 what sort of money was used as currency where they lived. But the Board was not particularly quick or competent in dealing with these matters and, moreover, not all consuls were keen to have to provide such information.

The Committee had its ups and downs, and long periods of inactivity, pilloried by Edmund Burke in his famous speech of 11 February 1780: *A plan for the better security of the independence of Parliament and the economical reformation of the civil and other establishments.* 'This board' he said, 'is a sort of temperate bed of influence; a sort of gently ripening hot-house, where eight members of Parliament receive salaries of a thousand a year, for a certain given time, in order to mature at a proper season, a claim to two thousand, granted for doing less, and on the credit of having toiled so long in that inferior laborious department ... This' he continued, 'is the history of the regeneration of the Board of Trade. It has perfectly answered its purposes. It was intended to quiet the minds of the people … the courtiers were too happy to be able to substitute a board, which they knew would be useless, in the place of one that they feared would be dangerous. Thus the Board of Trade was reproduced in a job; and perhaps it is the only instance of a public body, which has never degenerated; but to this hour preserves all the health and vigour of its primitive institution'.

William Eden, a member of the Board, attempted to rebut this attack by giving an outline of the Board's duties. Its proceedings consisted of answers and reports to the Houses of Parliament, representations addressed immediately to the King, reports to the Privy Council, correspondence with the Secretaries of State, with the Treasury, with foreign consuls, with governors and civil officers in the plantations, with corporate bodies and with individuals. He said that the Board had done material service in improving the coinage, in introducing many useful laws respecting all the principal branches of trade, in opening many branches of commerce, in examining all new laws in the plantations, and performing many other duties. The Board would also appear to have had a distinguished supporter in George III who wrote to Lord North shortly after the debate in which Burke made his attack: 'Lord North: I am sorry Men should so far lose their reason and let the violence of the times or fears actuate them as to forget the utility of the Board of Trade'.

Nevertheless Burke had his way, and the Committee was abolished by the Civil List and Secret Service Money Act of 1782. By this, the Board and its offices 'shall be; and are hereby utterly suppressed and taken away'. The Board's duties and powers were divided between the Home Department and the Privy Council. But it

3. Civil List and Secret Service Money Act 1782, which abolished the old Board of Trade.

was clearly needed and was very soon reconstituted, first in 1784 by an Order in Council as a Committee of the Privy Council for the consideration of all matters relating to trade and foreign plantations, and again on 23 August 1786.

The Order of 1786, which is celebrated by the present history, remains in force to this day as the basic instrument from which the Department still derives its general authority as the department concerned with trade. Members of the new Board included the Archbishop of Canterbury, who is still a nominal member. (Churchill, when Chancellor, once had to reply to a question asking how often the Archbishop, as a member, had attended meetings of the Board of Trade. His alleged answer was: 'Save for the President himself, no member of the Board has been more assiduous in his attendance than his Grace the Archbishop.') Other members were the First Lords of the Treasury and Admiralty, the principal Secretaries of State, the Master of the Mint, Mr Speaker, the Chancellor of the Exchequer and a number of other public and private persons. (A complete list appears on page 119.) A further Order made the following day established a secretariat with 17 staff: a chief clerk at a salary of £500 per annum, seven other clerks, an office keeper and messengers, and 'one necessary woman' at £50 a year. The salaries of President and Vice-President were not to exceed £2,000. The Board's business was to consider commercial treaties, colonial acts affecting trade, import and export duties and prohibitions concerning trade.

In the 18th and early 19th centuries, the mode of doing business at the Board appears to have been by minutes passed at meetings consisting of all or some of the members. A memorandum of 1880 on the origin and authority of the Board states that 'From the minute books for the years between 1786 and 1797, it appears that members of the Committee varying from one to seven or eight actually attended, the President of the Board

4. A page of minutes of a meeting of the Board, 1789.

being always one, and sometimes acting alone. No quorum was required by the Order in Council and therefore the act of one member of the Board was sufficient. This mode of doing business, however, gradually became a fiction, and the business of the office came to be conducted as in other offices, by a single Minister of State aided by a permanent staff'. Letters were read and evidence taken, for the Board often acted as a committee of inquiry.

According to K A Mallaber (in BT 13/245) 'up to 1808 it was not uncommon for 4 or 5 members to attend meetings and as many as 7 or 8 names recur in the minute books, though there are occasions when the President and Vice-President only were present. The last member of the Committee apart from the President and Vice-President to attend regularly was Lord Redesdale (ex Speaker of the House of Commons, ex Lord Chancellor of Ireland) and the last meeting he attended was held on June 19, 1810.' The last recorded attendance of any other members was on 29 July 1821. The last recorded meeting of the Board as a collective entity (ie President and Vice-President) was on 23 December 1850. In 1853 the minute books were discontinued. The office of Vice-President was abolished in 1867 and a Parliamentary Secretary substituted. An answer given by the then President, Gerald Balfour, in Parliament on 15 March 1901 stated categorically: 'The Board of Trade does meet. The quorum consists of one person – myself.'

Despite many reorganisations, additions and subtractions, the Board of Trade, now transformed into today's DTI, has completed 200 years of continuous history. Several of the present Departments of government, for instance, Employment, Energy and Transport, had their beginnings as divisions of the Board before achieving independent status.

The Board of Trade and Commerce

THE reconstituted Board of Trade in 1786 had oversight of commercial treaties, colonial acts affecting trade, tariff negotiations with other countries, and the British tariff system. It was also in charge of assessing the country's food requirements and regulating the supply by restricting or relaxing import and export of corn under the corn laws.

The problems raised by the secession of the American colonies were subsequently to be compounded by war in Europe. The Napoleonic wars brought with them increasing worries for the Board, with responsibilities for navigation laws, the blockades and the provision of essential supplies. Corn supplies were scarce, and the price of bread rose to new heights during the wars. In 1812 wheat cost 126/6d a quarter, but by the end of the war in 1815 prices fell to 65/6d. Panic among landlords and farmers caused the rushing through of a corn law to keep the price artificially high. Eventually constant price fluctuations coupled with low wages led to demands from workers and the Anti-Corn Law League for repeal of the corn laws. This was finally achieved in 1846 by Sir Robert Peel's government with a package of measures abolishing duties on imported corn over three years.

'His Majesty's government have thought it more prudent and more dignified to enter into amicable arrangements with other powers, founded on the basis of mutal interest and entire reciprocity of advantages, rather than embark in a contest of commercial hostility and reciprocal exclusion'. William Huskisson, House of Commons, May 1826.

In 1820 a group of London merchants presented a petition to Parliament in favour of free trade. This was drafted by Thomas Tooke, a member of the Political Economy Club, a body of people interested in developing the science of economics, with a bias towards free trade. He won support from politicians like Lord Liverpool (as Lord Hawkesbury, President of the Board in 1786), Huskisson and Canning, but observed that 'the government were at that time far more sincere and resolute free traders than the merchants of London'. The Board of Trade had many supporters trying to convince politicians of the benefits of free trade. Committees of both Houses were set up and recommended many modifications to the old tariff structure. The Board had good relations with the public at that time, as can be seen from its reply to a letter from a representative of the woollen manufacturers, noted in the minutes of the meeting of 23 May 1822, saying that the Committee felt it 'to be their Duty at all times to receive with Attention the Representations of Individuals, as well as of Bodies of Men, who may be affected, or may be apprehensive of being affected by any particular Measure'.

The first determined effort to liberate trade from protectionist restrictions was made by

The Blessings of Peace or the Curse of the Corn Bill.

Huskisson when President from 1823 to 1827. He was aided in this by James Deacon Hume, a surveyor of Customs who subsequently became joint Assistant Secretary of the Board. In 1825 Huskisson laid before Parliament 10 bills consolidating the existing revenue laws. Hume edited the acts with notes and indexes. For his labours he was given a public grant of £6,000, which he, alas, lost through a bad investment. Speaking in the House of Commons in May 1826, on the relaxation of the navigation laws, Huskisson said that the peace with America in 1783 'gave the first blow to the navigation system of this country … that part of the system which provided that none of the productions of Asia, Africa or America should be imported into England except in British vessels, could no longer be adhered to … In the long run, this war of discriminating duties … must operate most to the injury of the country which, at the time of entering upon it, possesses the greatest mercantile marine. How can it be otherwise? What are these discriminating duties but a tax upon commerce and navigation? Will not the heaviest share of that

6. William Huskisson, President of the Board of Trade 1823–1827.

7. Free trade.

8. Postcards depicting the nations that took advantage of Britain's lifting of protectionist restrictions.

tax fall, therefore, upon those who have the greatest amount of shipping and of trade?'

Huskisson's outstanding achievements as President have been summarised by Anna Lane Lingelbach as helping to 'bring order out of the chaos of laws that were stifling trade, commerce and even industry, to encourage shipping but at the same time free it from prohibitions … to free raw materials and then provide wider markets with less protection for manufactured goods; and to establish reciprocity with other nations'. Huskisson's reductions of tariff and partial abolition of the navigation laws were both based on the principle of reciprocity; this being to extend to all countries willing to act on the principle, equality of duties and drawbacks on goods imported in the ships of those countries into the United Kingdom.

Subsequent negotiations were mainly carried out by the Board acting as adviser to the Foreign Office. In 1840 the Committee on Import Duties came out strongly against protection. Board of Trade officials had ensured this by supplying most of the evidence and being questioned by convinced free-trade MPs who packed the Committee. In 1842 the second major revision of the tariff was accomplished by Sir Robert Peel's government and, again, the detailed work was chiefly performed by the Board. A revised sliding scale was introduced, designed to reduce the incentive to hoard grain. Duties on colonial coffee and timber were lowered and the import of livestock and provisions permitted. Duties were reduced on 750 dutiable articles and the resultant loss of revenue made up by a temporary tax of 7d

9. William Gladstone, Vice-President of the Board of Trade 1841–1843, President 1843–1845.

in the £ on incomes above £150 a year. Gladstone was then Vice-President and afterwards declared that, of all the four tariff revisions with which he had been concerned, the first one was six times as laborious as the other three put together. A further revision followed in 1845, which was the last in which the Board had a leading role, the Treasury taking the initiative thereafter. After that the Board's fiscal and commercial work was greatly reduced, although it continued to monitor colonial tariffs and collect trade statistics.

The Board's main functions, which had formerly been to act as adviser to the government or other departments on problems of trade and industry, gave way in the mid-19th century to largely executive duties. These included work concerned with the new Railway and Marine departments, the collection of statistics and registration of joint stock companies. The Board did, however, take an active part in negotiation of the 1860 Cobden treaty with France on tariffs and free trade. Then, in 1864, a select committee was appointed to 'inquire into the arrangement between the Foreign Office and the Board of Trade with reference to the trade with foreign nations' but could not decide which department should be wholly responsible for commercial negotiations. Its eventual recommendations were a compromise but the Foreign Office had pre-empted the decision by creating its own commercial department to which in 1872 the consultative business of the Board's Commercial department was transferred, together with the old library. The remains of the consultative business were amalgamated with the Board's Statistical department, and included the work of recording changes in foreign and colonial tariffs and of collecting trade statistics.

As the Board alone possessed the essential data relating to trade and tariff changes, in 1882 its

Marche triomphale de MM. Cobden Brigth et Gibson

10. Messrs Cobden, Bright (President of the Board of Trade 1868–1870), and Milner-Gibson (President of the Board of Trade, 1859–1866). Cartoon by Daumier, 1856.

Commercial department was once more recognised as the Foreign Office's official adviser on commercial policy. During Joseph Chamberlain's presidency officials were encouraged to form close ties with representative bodies such as chambers of commerce. (It was chambers of commerce and trades councils of many sorts that wrote to the Board in 1905 in a campaign to establish a Ministry of Commerce, although nothing came of this.) In 1886 the demand for a convenient source of official intelligence culminated with the publication of the *Board of Trade Journal*. This supplied its readers with a mass of information, mainly from official sources, on movements of overseas trade, tariff changes, consular reports on the trade of various countries, and news of export opportunities.

A Trade and Treaties Committee was set up in 1890, under the chairmanship of Anthony Mundella, a past President of the Board, to watch the cycle of commercial negotiations on the continent which resulted in the Caprivi Treaties of 1891–94. The Committee drew up a series of reports dealing with tariff and commercial relations with France, Central European countries and Spain. In 1897 a permanent Commercial Intelligence branch was created within the Commercial department to act as a clearing-house for official information and initiate inquiries in overseas markets as to openings for trade, and to

THE COLONIAL CONFERENCE

MR W A ROBINSON   MR T W HOLDERNESS   SIR W LYNE   SIR W BAILLIE HAMILTON
RT HON WINSTON CHURCHILL M.P. SIR T HOPWOOD GENERAL BOTHA MR H W JUST MR G W JOHNSON SIR J MACKAY HON L P BRODEUR   SIR R BOND
RT HON H ASQUITH M.P.   SIR J WARD   SIR W LAURIER   LORD ELGIN   HON A DEAKIN HON F R MOOR RT HON LLOYD GEORGE M.P.

11. The Colonial Conference, 1907.

disseminate information to the business world.

The colonial conference of 1907 adopted a resolution in favour of representation of British trade interests in the Dominions by permanent trade commissioners. These posts were established the following year and the trade commissioners' duties were to assist British trade by answering queries from traders or the parent department, helping British trade visitors, keeping abreast with local commercial and industrial conditions, and reporting promptly on topics of interest. They also produced an annual review of commercial conditions in their own districts, and so had to travel widely and also pay periodic visits to the United Kingdom. By 1914 the salaries of the trade commissioners in Canada and South Africa were £1,000 pa, in New Zealand £800 and in Australia £1,100. Their work was investigated by the Royal Commission on Dominions trade which, in 1917, recommended an extension of the system with commercial attaches jointly controlled by the Foreign Office and the Board of Trade. Immediately after World War I, India, East Africa and the West Indies were brought within the scope of the trade commissioner service. Control eventually passed to the joint Department of Overseas Trade which completed the reorganisation of the service and created a new Commercial Diplomatic Service. This passed much information to the Board on customs tariffs and foreign legislation and administration affecting trade. In 1919 the Commercial department of the Board was renamed the Commercial Relations and Treaties department, and took part in a number of commercial negotiations and international conventions. The counterpart of the Board's Overseas Trade divisions was, in a sense, the trade commissioner service in commonwealth countries and the Commercial Diplomatic Service, under the

12.   Sir W H Clark, Comptroller General, Department of Overseas Trade in the early 1920s.

Foreign Office, in other foreign countries – the 'eyes, ears and voice of the Board of Trade abroad'.

The British Overseas Trade Board

The Board of Trade had, from its earliest days, been concerned with the import and export of goods. Overseas trade, especially during William Huskisson's presidency when the navigation laws were relaxed and free trade promoted, was a topic of constant importance, just as it is today. In the 20th century, even before the first world war had ended, a combined Foreign Office/Board of Trade

Department of Overseas Trade was given delegated power to carry on the work of collecting and disseminating commercial intelligence and administering the commercial services abroad. In 1946 this Department was absorbed into the Board of Trade.

The British Overseas Trade Board was set up in January 1972 to promote British exports and help exporters. Its president is the Secretary of State for Trade and Industry, and its members are drawn mainly from industry and commerce.

13. BOTB aid to exporters.

This was part of the Heath government's policy of involving business leaders in public administration and bringing their expertise into government. BOTB advises the government on overseas trade strategy, directs and develops the government's export promotion services and encourages and supports industry and commerce in their overseas trade activities. The services provide a wide range of market advice, help with regulatory and technical requirements, and practical and financial help for getting into overseas markets.

In 1982 the Commercial Relations and Export Services activities were brought together into headquarters at 1 Victoria Street. The new set-up provides a unified specialist service responsive to the needs of the exporting community. Help is available direct from the Market Branches at headquarters or from the ten Regional Offices throughout the UK.

EXPORT CREDITS GUARANTEE DEPARTMENT

ECGD was set up as a sub-department of the Department of Overseas Trade in 1919, after the disruption of Britain's export trade by the first world war when overseas customers were forced to look elsewhere for the goods which Britain could no longer provide. The Board of Trade was empowered to grant credits and undertake insurances 'for the purpose of re-establishing overseas trade' under the Overseas Trade (Credits and Insurance) Act 1920. In the same year the first advisory committee (now a council) of businessmen and bankers was set up. In 1921 a system of guaranteeing bills drawn by traders for exports was introduced. In 1930 ECGD became an independent department with its own Vote. Subsequently, during World War II, ECGD became involved in substantial claims, in respect of both Germany and Poland, from its comprehensive policyholders, and there was increased demand for transfer cover on other countries that might have their communications with the UK upset through war. By the end of 1940, when the 'export or die' drive was at its peak, British exporters had a wide choice of policies covering most risks. In March 1941 the United States Congress passed its Lend-Lease Act and so removed some of the urgent need to earn dollars. At the same time restrictions were placed on the export of goods to many countries, except where they were of direct aid to the war effort.

Today ECGD insures over one-third of Britain's exports, to a value of over £13,000 million a year, and has around 12,000 exporters on its books. It has close links with the Department of Trade and Industry, but has intentionally been made independent. It is essentially a business organisation with its primary concern that of providing insurance cover for exporters against default and transfer risks, to banks for export finance, insurance against political risks on new overseas investment, and so on.

R E P O R T

OF

The Lords of the Committee of Council appointed for the Confideration of all Matters relating to Trade and Foreign Plantations;

SUBMITTING TO HIS MAJESTY'S CONSIDERATION

The EVIDENCE and INFORMATION they have collected in confequence of his MAJESTY's Order in Council, dated the 11th of February 1788, concerning the prefent State of the Trade to AFRICA, and particularly the Trade in SLAVES; and concerning the Effects and Confequences of this Trade, as well in AFRICA and the WEST INDIES, as to the general Commerce of this Kingdom.

1789.

14.   Board of Trade report on the slave trade, 1789.

SLAVE TRADE

The slave trade from Liverpool had begun in 1709 and was highly profitable. It traded in slaves from Africa to the West Indies and the American plantations. There was reasoned opposition to this in the United Kingdom from the first, particularly in non-conformist circles. The Committee for Trade and Plantations carried out a major study of the slave trade which drew on the testimony of merchants trading in Africa, of colonial agents, and of ministers abroad, regarding the state of the African trade as carried out by foreign countries, and evidence from those who knew about the transportation of slaves to the colonies and their treatment there. The number of slaves annually carried from the coast of Africa in British vessels was estimated to be 38,000, while the number carried annually to the British West India Islands was about 22,500. The number annually retained in the West Indies, according to Customs House accounts was around 17,500. All these approximate figures are given in the report. Part two dealt with slave-ships, provisions, officers, and the mortality of both slaves and seamen.

The report, which had taken over a year to produce, was published in March 1789 and presented to the House by Pitt that April. Its evidence formed the basis for two of Wilberforce's great speeches on abolition. However, Lord Hawkesbury, then President of the Board (and later Earl of Liverpool) made a lukewarm speech in the Lords in 1792, favouring regulation rather than abolition. He said abolition would injure commercial interests, the navigation and the revenue of the country, and so the Lords should consider justice as well as humanity. The campaign met with little success until 1807 when a Bill was tabled for abolition of the slave trade.

Huskisson, in his speech given in May 1826 on the navigation laws, referred to this appalling trade and the attitude of the Parliament of the day, when he remarked 'The arguments in opposition to the measure were grounded chiefly on the danger with which it threatened the shipping interest of the country. The necessity of kidnapping cargoes of slaves on the coast of Africa was at that time, as coolly defended, on the score of encouragement to our marine as the taking of cod-fish on the banks of Newfoundland could be at the present day.'

After abolition of the African trade, the Duke of Wellington joined in a protest against the West India Slavery (Abolition) Bill 1833 on the grounds that the slaves were unprepared for their new social position! Wilberforce pointed out in reply that emancipation alone would prepare them. Even after the slave trade had been abolished throughout the British colonies, ships still continued to transport Africans across the Atlantic and Britain now pursued an active policy of suppression; British captains making a practice of taking slaves aboard their own ships to free them.

BOARD OF TRADE AND STATISTICS

In 1832, when the main functions of the Board were still consultative rather than executive, the statistics-gathering work was the first to be organised as a separate department, which also included the Corn Office. The Board had collected trade statistics for a long time but had not the means to consolidate and present the figures except in its minute books and other manuscript volumes.

The new department was directed by G R Porter (later, author of *The Progress of the Nation*).

15. Lord Hawkesbury (later Earl of Liverpool). First President of the newly-constituted Board of Trade, 1786–1804.

16. Wellington's protest against the abolition of slavery.

17.   G R Porter, first director of the Statistics department of the Board of Trade, 1832, and Permanent Secretary 1847–52.

18.   Robert Giffen, appointed chief of the Statistical department of the Board of Trade, and Comptroller of corn returns, in 1876.

He instituted a statistical year book entitled *Tables of the revenue, population, commerce, etc of the United Kingdom and its dependencies*. Porter later incorporated *The accounts of trade and navigation,* which had originated around 1830, in his year book. In 1894, during the Presidency of Edward (later Viscount) Cardwell, the publication of statistics was reorganised. The year book was subdivided into a number of more specialised returns and abstracts which, over a period of years, included statistical abstracts of the United Kingdom, of the colonies, of foreign countries, railway statistics, cotton statistics, foreign import duties and special tariff returns. An Act of 1828

had given the Board of Trade direct control over the Comptroller of corn returns, who supervised the collection of prices upon which the sliding scale which determined the corn duty depended. After his office was abolished, the Statistics department continued to collect statutory returns of the sale and prices of corn in a large number of markets. This task was transferred to the new Board of Agriculture in 1892.

Throughout the years the Statistics department and the Board's Library have been closely connected. In fact, the Statistics department had a library almost from its inception, and the post of Librarian to the Board of Trade was originally created in 1843. In 1872 the Statistics department was united with the old Commercial department of the Board. Robert Giffen was appointed chief of the Statistical department and Comptroller of corn returns. He extended the range of activities considerably, arranging for his staff to handle statistics of trade, shipping and railways. In 1893 a separate Labour branch was created within the department, and the *Labour Gazette* was published to give up-to-date information on employment and wages in the United Kingdom and abroad. Reports were issued on changes in wages and hours of work, strikes, trade unions, unemployment and, in 1903, the first report on wholesale and retail prices. This was the starting point of the Board of Trade index of wholesale prices and indices of retail prices and the cost of living, which are still in being today.

The 1906 Census of Production Act, introduced by David Lloyd George when President, imposed on the Board the duty of taking a periodical census of the industrial production of the United Kingdom, and a special Census Office was established as part of the Commercial, Labour and Statistical department. The first census was taken in 1908 and covered production by small and large establishments during 1907. The Act specified that information should be obtained about the nature of the trade, output, number of working days, number of employees and power used or generated. The Import Duties Act 1932 extended powers to collect information about industries affected under the Act. The Statistics of Trade Act 1947 empowered information to be collected on, among other things, the nature of employment, pay, quantity and value of output, capital expenditure, orders, stocks and work in progress. In addition to providing for short period statistics, the Act required the Board to take a census of production for 1949 and every year thereafter, and a census of distribution and other services in any year prescribed by the Board.

In 1953 the then President appointed a Committee to advise him about future policy on censuses of production and distribution. The Committee recommended certain changes to make them more effective and reduce the burden imposed on the business community. A wider range of small firms were exempted from the obligation to complete detailed returns. There was much criticism in the 1950s and 1960s of the lack of a range of business statistics capable of monitoring changes in the British economy. The fourth report from the House of Commons Estimates Committee 1966–67 called for more timely and detailed industrial statistics. The response of the Government Statistical Service was to announce the creation of the Business Statistics Office (BSO) with responsibility for collecting and publishing industrial statistics and for developing business registers.

19.   Business Statistics Office, Newport, Gwent.

The Business Statistics Office at Newport began operating in 1969 and took over the work previously carried out by the former Census Office at Eastcote. The Office's main function had been to carry out the large-scale censuses of production and distribution at five or ten-year intervals, supported by a range of official business statistics covering periods between censuses. BSO moved in stages to Newport and by 1972 it was located in purpose-built offices. By the mid-1970s

BSO and the statistical divisions of the Department had designed and implemented a new system of industrial statistics with short-term, annual and less frequent inquiries to business and a system of annual inquiries to distribution and service industries.

Since 1979, with rising concern about public expenditure, the volume of information collected and the number of staff have been reduced. BSO's statistical output involves use of both statutory and voluntary inquiries. In 1984 BSO sent out 356,000 forms of which about 162,000 were statutory requests and 194,000 associated with voluntary inquiries. BSO is now working on an extended Census of Production and detailed inquiry into industrial purchases of materials and fuel for the year 1984.

The Department of Trade and Industry also compiles overseas trade statistics and, until the transfer of Marine division to the Department of Transport in 1983, shipping and navigation

20.   Statistics & Market Intelligence Library, when at Export House.

statistics. All these, and other published government statistical series may be seen at the Department's Statistics and Market Intelligence Library, originally located at Export House near St. Paul's Cathedral, with the export divisions, and now with them in headquarters at 1 Victoria Street. This library also holds major collections of overseas statistical publications, overseas trade directories and foreign development plans. British businessmen and exporters can use this material for reference and for desk research on overseas markets.

SOLICITOR'S DEPARTMENT

The legal aspects of the Board's work were dealt with by the Customs and Excise solicitor until 1868, when a law officer was added to the staff. In 1875 a solicitor was appointed and in 1877 the present Solicitor's department was formed with the addition of four solicitor's clerks. Its responsibilities today include the drafting of subordinate legislation, litigation arising in relation to Acts, Regulations and Orders administered by the Department of Trade and Industry, conduct of prosecutions and the issuing of instructions to Parliamentary Counsel for the preparation of legislation sponsored by the Department.

BOARD OF TRADE JOURNAL

The *Board of Trade Journal* was first published in September 1886. Its full title was *The Board of Trade Journal of Tariff and Trade Notices and Miscellaneous Commercial Information* and it appeared monthly,

THE
Board of Trade Journal
OR

TARIFF AND TRADE NOTICES

AND

MISCELLANEOUS COMMERCIAL INFORMATION.

Vol. I.]   July—August 1886.   [No. 1.

INTRODUCTORY NOTE.

THE primary object of the Board of Trade in instituting a Journal is to provide a vehicle for conveying to the public in a convenient form information as to Tariffs for which the *Gazette* is hardly a suitable form of publication, and for which the present Import Duties Returns, published at long intervals, are also in part unsuitable: the necessary delay, moreover, in publishing the latter returns making part of the information less useful to the public than it would otherwise be. The form of a Journal, it has been found, will be most convenient for the purpose in view, principally to give full information as to Tariff changes and information as to Customs regulations and Customs decisions as to the interpretation of Tariffs which are frequently more material to merchants than the Tariffs themselves.

With this object it is also proposed to combine an attempt to give the public information of trade movements abroad of which the Government obtain knowledge through Her Majesty's representatives abroad, or through

A 2

[23460.

21.   First issue of the *Board of Trade Journal,* 1886.

price 6d. A leader in *The Times* greeted its birth with some pleasure: 'The commercial importance of this new official enterprise can hardly be exaggerated ... It is only right that such information on commercial topics as the Government collects or receives should be placed unreservedly and with all reasonable despatch at the service of the general community ... Its fair prospect must not be marred by an untoward striving after economy.' The editor of the *Journal,* 75 years later, wrote that 'the decision to publish ... was a milestone of some consequence to commerce. It marked a change in the Government's conception of the proper function of the Board of Trade. To its traditional

regulatory functions was now added a responsibility for providing an intelligence service for British exporters and for collecting and publishing statistics of working population and unemployment.'

The *Journal* was born in a period of anxiety about trade at home and abroad. Britain was faced with increasing foreign competition and dumping of surplus goods, and had difficulty in penetrating protectionist markets overseas. Export values stagnated between the early 1870s until nearly the turn of the century and the deficit in visible trade grew. In 1881 the 'Fair Trade League', which campaigned against dumping and for retaliation against overseas protectionism, won some publicity and support. Evidence given to the Royal Commission set up in 1885 to examine 'the causes of the depression in trade and industry' showed that the *laissez faire* attitude of British diplomacy towards foreign trade was out of date and that information on commercial matters sent from abroad was not of the right kind, arrived too late and was not published in accessible and attractive form. The Commission also said 'in the course of our inquiry we have frequently experienced the want of accurate statistics with regard to the details of our home trade.' The founding of the *Journal* went at least some way towards remedying these matters.

History is seen afresh in these pages. Scanning the index for, say, 1893, we find: Restrictions on imports of firearms in Lagos; vaccination of crews of vessels in the Great Lakes; the status of aliens in the United States; Russian competition with English trade in China. The *Journal* refers to a Committee set up in May 1912, soon after the *Titanic* sank, to look into the internal subdivision of vessels of all classes by watertight bulkheads and other means, in the interests of safety of life at sea. In 1914 there is an item on the prohibition of the export of 'warlike stores' from the UK and a warning on trading with the enemy.

In January 1918 the physical format of the *Journal* was increased to approximately today's dimensions and the price of each issue (published weekly since 1900 at one penny) rose again to 6d. The title was changed to the *Board of Trade and Commercial Gazette* and, although the war was not yet over, a big export drive was being planned by a combined Foreign Office/Board of Trade Department of Overseas Trade (Development and Intelligence). The *Journal's* scope was to be widened to include articles dealing generally with all the activities of the Board of Trade and the Department of Overseas Trade.

Between the wars the *Journal* continued to register movements of trade and opportunities for exporters. In World War II it recorded changes in administrative controls – clothes rationing, utility schemes, price controls. After the war there was increased preoccupation with the need to expand exports, conversion of arms factories to civilian production, and regional development in areas of heavy unemployment. The *Journal* changed its name to *Trade and Industry* after the amalgamation of the Board of Trade and Ministry of Technology in 1970, and again in 1980 to *British business*, a title designed to reflect its growing role as a vehicle for promoting British products in home and overseas markets.

Although much altered in appearance in recent years, the *Journal* continues to provide a wide range of export and industrial information from the Department of Trade and Industry. But there have been changes in content in response to the new information requirements of the readership. The statistics section has been expanded and there is now weekly coverage of developments in the European Community. Other new features include in-depth reports on export opportunities

22.   *In business now*, sister publication to *British business*, first published in 1983.

in Britain's major markets and regular profiles of successful British companies and their technological achievements.

In September 1983 *British business* gave birth to another publication — *In business now* — a free bi-monthly tabloid newspaper aimed specifically at small and growing businesses.

COMPANIES

The South Sea Bubble affair – that episode of speculative mania and ensuing financial disaster for many – had discredited joint stock companies and they were prohibited by the 'Bubble Act' of 1719. This remained in force for over a century, and up to 1825 the formation of such companies, except by private Acts of Parliament, was still banned. The Bubble Act was repealed in that year by an Act conferring greater power on the Crown in granting incorporating charters and declaring that a charter could prescribe individual liability on company members. The Trading Companies Act 1834, brought in by the President Poulett

Thomson, had enabled the King to 'invest trading and other companies with the powers necessary for the due conduct of their affairs and for the security of the rights and interests of their creditors'. But, with the advent of free trade and the boom in business after the Industrial Revolution, large sums of money had to be raised, most of it by small investors. Use of a joint stock fund was made available to all; one or more people could form a company or corporation and, after registering with the Board of Trade and meeting certain requirements, could sell stock to the public.

Board of Trade presidents had long been accustomed to advise governments on the granting of charters of incorporation to companies. Committees had studied various aspects of company law and finance, and an 1843 inquiry recommended that the Board should set up an office especially for the registration of companies. Agitation by Poulett Thomson (he later became Lord Sydenham), President in 1834 and 1835 and subsequently Gladstone (Vice-President and President 1841–45) paved the way for the passing of the Joint Stock Companies Act 1844. This

23.   C Poulett Thomson (later Lord Sydenham). President of the Board of Trade 1834, 1835–1839.

24.   First annual report.

REPORT

BY THE

REGISTRAR OF JOINT-STOCK COMPANIES

IN THE

COMMITTEE

OF

PRIVY COUNCIL FOR TRADE.

Pursuant to the 7 and 8 Vict. c. 110, s.19.

FOR THE YEAR

1845.

LONDON,
PRINTED BY W. CLOWES AND SONS, STAMFORD STREET,
FOR HER MAJESTY'S STATIONERY OFFICE.
1846.

25. The collapse of the South Sea Bubble.

required all such companies to register with a registrar appointed by and answerable to the Board of Trade. The intention of the Act was to safeguard companies, shareholders and creditors.

Huskisson had mentioned the question of limited liability in the Bubble Act repeal debate, and it was finally conferred by registration in the Limited Liability Act 1855. This was repealed in the following year and replaced by the 1856 Joint Stock Companies Act by which seven or more people could, by registering a memorandum of association, become a body corporate with limited liability.

By 1862 2,479 companies had registered, whereas in 1844 there had been only 994. Companies on the register at 31 December 1983 in England and Wales totalled 956,411 (of which over 100,000 were in liquidation or in course of removal). In 1904 the Companies department of the Board was established under a comptroller.

He had oversight of assurance and insurance companies, partnerships, sections of the Moneylenders Act 1900, registration and winding-up of companies, changes of business name, filing of annual returns of registered companies and regulation of limited liability. Successive Acts kept pace with changes in the business environment, and all details of companies, including their annual accounts, were filed at Companies House in London. In 1976 most of the work of the Companies Registration Office began to move from London to Cardiff. There is also an office in Edinburgh.

The present-day Financial Services and Companies division deals also with matters affecting the commercial competitiveness of the financial services sector, regulation of the securities industry, investor protection, the accountancy profession, and companies investigations.

26. Companies Registration Office, Cardiff

27. The Gower report

A departmental committee was appointed in February 1936 to consider what changes in existing law relating to the carrying-on of insurance business were desirable in the light of statutory provisions concerning compulsory insurance against third party risks and by employers against liability to their workmen. One of its main recommendations was that no insurer should be allowed to transact any class of compulsory insurance business unless licensed to do so by the Board of Trade.

After the war Sir Stafford Cripps, when moving the second reading of the then Assurance Companies Bill, explained that with the resumption of the ordinary business of assurance

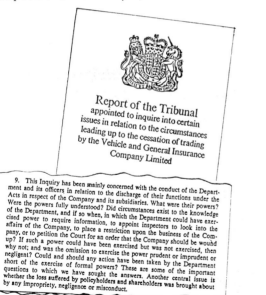

Report of the Tribunal appointed to inquire into certain issues in relation to the circumstances leading up to the cessation of trading by the Vehicle and General Insurance Company Limited

9. This Inquiry has been mainly concerned with the conduct of the Department and its officers in relation to the discharge of their functions under the Acts in respect of the Company and its subsidiaries. What were their powers? Were the powers fully understood? Did circumstances exist to the knowledge of the Department, and if so when, in which the Department could have exercised power to require information, to appoint inspectors to look into the affairs of the Company, to place a restriction upon the business of the Company, or to petition the Court for an order that the Company should be wound up? If such a power could have been exercised but was not exercised, then why not; and was the omission to exercise the power prudent or imprudent or negligent? Could and should any action have been taken by the Department short of the exercise of formal powers? These are some of the important questions to which we have sought the answers. Another central issue is whether the loss suffered by policyholders and shareholders was brought about by any impropriety, negligence or misconduct.

28. Page 3, paragraph 9 of the report on the Vehicle & General Insurance Company Ltd.

in the international field the Bill was needed because its main object was to ensure, as far as possible, that there would be no failures of British insurance companies in the future which would entail great losses to policyholders.

Even in a great Department of state, however, things can occasionally go wrong. The case of the Vehicle & General Insurance Company, which ceased trading in 1971 with the resultant inability to meet claims of and against policyholders and to honour obligations under unexpired policies, is well known. A tribunal was set up to inquire into certain relevant issues and reported in February 1972. It asked a number of pertinent questions (see picture 28).

Today the Insurance division administers the Insurance Companies Act 1982 which consolidated provisions of earlier Acts. It authorises and supervises insurance companies. The division is also concerned with general questions affecting the insurance industry (insurance companies, Lloyds, insurance brokers and other intermediaries) and with European Community and other international insurance matters.

BANKRUPTCY

When Joseph Chamberlain became President in 1880 he received a memorial from bankers and merchants in the City complaining about the current inadequate bankruptcy laws and administration and the increase of insolvency. The resulting Bankruptcy Act 1883 is still the basis of present-day bankruptcy administration. Its purpose, said Chamberlain, was 'to protect the salvage and also to diminish the number of wrecks'. Chamberlain described Robert Giffen, head of the Statistics department, as 'to a great

29. Joseph Chamberlain, President of the Board of Trade 1880–1885.

extent the real author of the measure' because he owed his own knowlege of the subject to Giffen. Before this Act came into being, the law relating to bankruptcy was concerned only with punishment of fraudulent bankrupts and protection of creditors. There was no provision for the release of a debtor from his obligations. In earlier times punishment had been brutal; the penalty prescribed by the 1623 Act for non-disclosure of his property by the bankrupt was to be 'set upon the pillory in some publick place for the space of two hours and to have one of his or her ears nailed to the pillory and cut off'.

The 1883 Act transferred to the Board of Trade all administrative functions previously carried out, not very efficiently, by the Courts. The Bankruptcy department was set up in the same year. It exercised general supervision and control over the Official Receivers attached to Courts in England and Wales which had bankruptcy jurisdiction. All companies ordered by the Court to be compulsorily wound up were under the supervision of the Board of Trade office in Carey Street – a name which quickly became synonymous with bankruptcy – and of Official Receivers under the provisions of the Companies Acts. The public officer by whom the investigation into the circumstances of bankruptcy was carried out was known as the Official Receiver. He acted under the direction of the Board and the Act recognised that bankruptcy was a matter affecting the community at large, so it provided that in all proceedings under the Act, the debtor should have his affairs examined and reported on by the Official Receiver, be subject to the supervision of the courts and should undergo a public examination. Now these officials protect the interests of creditors and assets of debtors against whom receiving orders are made, investigate the conduct and affairs of debtors and frequently become trustees of bankrupts' estates.

The framework of the present system was established in the latter half of the 19th century and has remained more or less intact with only a few minor alterations. No major reform was carried out until the passing of the 1976 Insolvency Act, although a new Insolvency Act received Royal Assent in October, 1985. The insolvency service now manages all aspects of insolvency procedure, including administration of the Official Receivers service in the High Court and provincial offices, supervision of liquidators and trustees, accounting for and management of funds, and insolvency matters affected by European Community legislation.

Railways, Tubes and Waterways

THE development of the railways coincides with the growth of factories and cities, and the effects of the Industrial Revolution; throughout the 19th century and into the 20th, the Board of Trade was concerned with the development and regulation of the railways. In 1786, the year the Board was reconstituted by Pitt, and in following years, a number of rail and tramways were constructed, usually for local collieries and workings, under the authority of private Acts.

The first scheme to be approved for a public use railway was that for the Stockton and Darlington line. In 1826 the bill was passed for the Liverpool-Manchester railway, with the enthusiastic backing of William Huskisson, then President of the Board. He argued that the canal monopoly exploited merchants and manufacturers wanting food and raw materials transported from Liverpool to the inland towns, and that cotton took longer to get to the Manchester mills from Liverpool than it took to reach Liverpool from New Orleans. The bill was delayed for four years due to Parliamentary obstruction. The prospectus for the Liverpool-Manchester line talked persuasively of the 'importance, to a commercial state, of a safe and cheap mode of transit for merchandise from one part of the country to another … this was the plea, upon the first introduction of canals: it was for the public advantage'.

> 'The province of the Board of Trade is to control, not to manage railways'
> *Westminster Review,* 1844, *XLII,* p60.

The railway was built and a competition held to find a suitable locomotive to run upon it, which was won by Stephenson's *Rocket* on 14 October 1829 at Rainhill. Huskisson went to

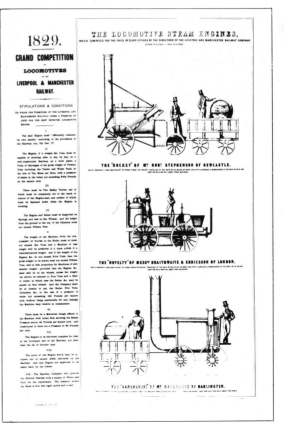

30. Poster advertising 1829 competition.

31. This cartoon, by Hugh Hughes (1790–1863) refers to the accident that befell William Huskisson, and is also a warning of the dangers of the railway. Here Huskisson is replaced by a tramp with a wooden leg. The locomotive shown, 'Northumbrian', took Huskisson to the nearest surgeon.

The Pleasures of the Rail-Road. — Caught in the Railway?

Liverpool in September 1830 for the opening of the Liverpool-Manchester railway. He was accident-prone, being slightly lame due to dislocating his ankle in 1801, had broken his arm three times, and seems to have been clumsy and lacking in agility. At the opening ceremony a procession of trains was run from Liverpool. When the engines stopped at Parkside for water, the passengers were standing on the track, contrary to instructions, when the *Rocket* approached them. The others climbed back into the carriage, but Huskisson lost his balance and fell on to the rails in front of the *Rocket*. The engine ran over his leg and he died 'in great agony' nine hours later. Thus, a former President of the Board of Trade, and one who was instrumental in the development of the railway, became the first victim of a form of transport which was to open new frontiers all over the world.

The number of railway projects submitted to Parliament over the next few years proliferated to such an extent that an appeal was made to the

32. President's room, Railway Board. 'The rooms devoted to railway business are profusely furnished with maps, projections, surveys, sections, models of every part of the United Kingdom.' *Illustrated London News*, 19 April 1845, p 249.

33. Offices of the Board of Trade, Whitehall. 'In consequence of the great increase of the business of the Board of Trade, and more especially since the establishment of the Railway Board ... it has been resolved to provide increased accommodations, by completing the design of the late Sir John Soane ...' *Illustrated London News*, 8 March 1845, p 153.

then President, Poulett Thomson, for guidance. In 1838 a Committee was appointed to see 'whether the powers which had been entrusted to the railroads by Parliament had been advantageously exercised and whether any amendment could be made'. The Committee recommended that control of the railways should be vested in a Board to be annexed to the Board of Trade; this was the inception of the Railway department, established in 1840.

Surprisingly enough, Gladstone, that arch-apostle of economic liberalism, did not rule out nationalisation of the railways. His 1844 Act contained powers for the state to buy out the railway companies when their charters ran out in 1860. It also imposed other regulations, including a fixed fare for third class travel that could only be raised with Parliament's consent – the so-called 'Parliamentary' trains. Companies deriving one-third or more of their revenue from passengers were to run one such train on every weekday at a speed of not less than 12 miles an hour, and the fare was not to exceed one penny a mile.

1844 saw the start of 'railway mania' and the rise of the speculators, among them 'King' Hudson, who made their fortunes by starting fraudulent companies and speculating in railway shares. The railway functions of the Board of Trade were transferred to an independent board of Railway Commissioners in 1846 and for the next five years the Board of Trade had little connection with railways. In 1847 the railway

34. George Hudson MP, the 'Railway King'.

35. Railway mania as the closing date for deposit of railway plans for the session of 1846 approaches.

bubble burst. A vivid picture of the ensuing Parliamentary debate of March 1848 is painted by Hubert Llewellyn Smith, 'when one speaker after another stood in a white sheet to apologise for the error made in taking away the work from the Board of Trade ... arch-speculator Hudson, the ''railway king'' in chastened mood, cried ''Why not send the business to the Board of Trade at once?'''. However, the Board's railway responsibilities were not restored until 1851.

A report in the *Daily Telegraph* of 1 September 1860 reads: 'The first street railway in Great Britain was opened on Thursday at Birkenhead ... the vehicles ... will accommodate from 20 to 30 inside passengers and about the same number of outsiders ... Two horses are used to each car: and it is said that a speed of 7 or 8 miles an hour can

36. Street railway-carriage at Birkenhead, 1860.

37. Stations on the Metropolitan Railway Line route, 1862.

be kept up without distress to the animals or real injury to the roadway'.

In London, the Metropolitan Railway opened to the public in January 1863 – the line running from Paddington to Farringdon Street – after its final inspection by Colonel Yolland on behalf of the Board of Trade. It was extended westward to Hammersmith in 1864 and east to Moorgate in the following year. Its inauguration coincided with renewed activity in promoting railways in London, again checked by a monetary crisis in 1866 when the great discount house of Overend Gurney failed for more than £5 million, and the Bank of England had to pay out £4 million to prop up liquidity as a result. It was the worst financial crash since 1825.

A joint Committee of both Houses of Parliament later inquired into the whole railway position; its report (largely drafted by the then Permanent Secretary to the Board, Thomas Farrer) was issued in 1872. The Committee felt that amalgamation of companies was inevitable and largely in the public interest. Takeovers had earlier drastically reduced the large number of companies of 1843 to about a score of regional groups by 1850. 'Few cases' the Committee concluded, 'have been adduced in which amalgamations already effected have led to increased fares or reduced facilities'. Thereafter the Board concentrated its attention on safeguarding the public against possible dangers arising from amalgamation, and dealing with problems of railway rates and classification. Its powers then related mainly to the safety of the travelling public and the welfare of railway employees. The Railway department inquired into accidents, investigated complaints as to hours of work of railway servants, looked after level crossings and inspected light railways and tramways.

In 1919 responsibility for railways passed to the new Ministry of Transport.

38. Railway
accident near
Salisbury, 1884.

39. Manchester Ship Canal, Irlam Locks, 1893.

40. The double lock and East entrance to the Islington Tunnel, Regent's Canal.

Canals, bridges and tunnels

The coming of the railways had a marked impact on canals, which had developed rapidly in the 18th century and had had a virtual monopoly on transport. Contemporary accounts speak of 110 vessels carrying timber, salt, coals and merchandise to the amount of 164,000 tons annually between Liverpool and Northwich and Winsford, of 42 boats of 50 tons on the Duke of Bridgewater's Canal making an average three trips to Liverpool every 14 days, and cargoes carried down by the Trent of lead, copper, coals and salt, cheese from Cheshire, Staffordshire ware, etc; and up, timber, hemp, flax, iron and groceries. In the 1820s cotton production had almost doubled, and Manchester's population risen accordingly. The need for efficient and relatively cheap transport of goods led to demand for an alternative to canals and, from the time of the development of the Stockton and Darlington railway onwards, they faced a strong challenge from rail.

Canals did not come under the jurisdiction of

41. The Board of Trade was doubly concerned with the Tay Bridge disaster, having responsibility for railway accidents *and* bridges.

the Board of Trade until 1854. But then the Board had to ensure that they were kept in good repair, inspect them when the works were in dangerous condition and issue warrants authorising abandonment of unnecessary or derelict canals.

Bridges were also part of these responsibilities. When the Tay Bridge collapsed as a train was crossing it in 1879, the Board of Trade convened a court of inquiry chaired by the Commissioner of Wrecks, and including among its members the Chief Inspecting Officer of Railways.

Most of the Board's powers relating to canals and bridges were vested in the new Minister of Transport appointed in 1919.

CHANNEL TUNNEL

The first proposal for a Channel Tunnel came from a French engineer in 1802. In the 1860s Sir John Hawkshaw and a French colleague produced plans for a railway tunnel. A pilot tunnel, 2,000 yards long, was bored near Folkestone in the early 1880s, but stopped after a press campaign against this 'security risk'. In 1960 a new study appeared and more negotiations and financial arrangements were undertaken. In 1964 the British government announced that the French and British had decided to proceed with a railway tunnel 'subject to further discussion of the legal and financial problems involved'. Trial borings began in 1974 but the British cancelled that project the following year due to rising costs. A UK/French study group was set up in 1981 to advise whether an acceptable scheme for a fixed cross-Channel link could be developed. It concluded that, if the market could raise the necessary finance, the best solution was one which combined a permanent link with a thriving maritime industry.

PUBLIC UTILITIES

The Board became responsible for coal mines in 1917. The Mining Industry Act 1920 ended the

42. Hopes and fears; or a dream of the Channel Tunnel, 1882.

Board's direct interest but a department of the Board of Trade, to be known as the Mines department was established. This was directed by a Parliamentary Secretary of the Board, who was referred to as the Secretary for Mines. All the powers and duties of the Board in relation to mines and the mining industry were to be exercised and performed through the Mines department, set up to secure 'the most effective development and utilisation of the mineral resources of the United Kingdom and the safety and welfare of those engaged in the mining industry'. The Mines department operated as a separate entity within the Board, being separately housed, with its own accounting and establishment officers. In 1942 the Mines department became part of the new Ministry of Fuel and Power.

The Board of Trade also carried out a number of duties in relation to public utility undertakings.

For example, it had administerial powers for the digging up of public roads for cables or pipes, for the carrying of wires and pipes over or under private property and for the supply of gas or water. Commercial supplies of gas began in the early 19th century and were sold on the basis of volume. Supplies were first subject to control under the 1847 Gas Works Clauses Act. Supply of electricity for light and power came later, and the first electric lighting act was passed in 1882 appropriately when Joseph Chamberlain was President. A Board of Electricity Commmissioners was established in 1919 and attached to the new Ministry of Transport. The Gas Act 1920 allowed the Board of Trade to make orders for a different method of charging — by therms.

The regulation of electricity, gas and water supply was dealt with by the Railway department until 1902, when administration was transferred to the Board's Harbour department. Gas supply eventually became part of the Board's Industries and Manufactures department, while responsibility for water was handed over to the Ministry of Health in 1920.

43. 1872 and the new electric lighting reaches the Thames Embankment.

44. The Board of Trade had powers over the supply of water in the 19th century.

The Telegraph Act 1863 regulated the exercise of powers under special acts for the construction and maintenance of telegraphs. The Board of Trade was responsible for hearing objections on works affecting streets and public roads, on private or Crown property, land or buildings, railways, canals and foreshores, and could appoint an arbitrator to solve disputes.

46.   General Post Office at Rathbone Street, London, in 1975.

45.   Examining the Atlantic telegraph cable after raising it. On board the *Great Eastern,* 1865.

However, it was not until April 1974 when the Ministry of Posts and Telecommunications was dissolved that its work was incorporated into the new Department of Industry, which was responsible for the Post Office and its consumer council, the Post Office Users National Council. British Telecom was hived off in October 1981 as a public corporation and privatised in August 1984, with the biggest share flotation in Britain, in November of that year. The government wished to encourage a wide spread of ownership of BT shares and took a number of special measures to ensure this. A share information office was set up to handle inquiries from the public and an

47.   Prospectus issued for sale of BT shares, 1984.

information pack provided. A network of stockbrokers was established to help in the communications programme and a national TV, radio and press campaign was mounted. Prospectuses were made widely available through banks and post offices, and there were special incentives in the form of free shares or telephone bill vouchers for individual investors.

The Board of Trade and Industry

THE Board of Trade has, during its life, been closely concerned with the manufacturing and service industries. As long ago as 1660, at the time of the Restoration of the Monarchy, the Council of Trade was instructed to 'consider the several manufactures of these our kingdoms, how and by what occasions they are corrupted, debased and disparaged. And by what probable means they may be restored and maintained in their ancient goodness and reputation'.

In 1789 the Committee for Trade and Plantations compiled a report on the corn trade.

> 'Ye are also to [consider] all the native commodities of the growth and production of these our kingdoms and how they may be ordered, nourished and manufactured to the employment of our people and to the best advantage of the publique.' *Instructions for the Council of Trade* appointed November 1660.

At various other times it reported on china and pottery, cotton, hemp and flax, gunpowder, dyeing materials, tin, leather and sugar. Inventions were encouraged and sometimes rewarded.

The general 'industrial' activities of the Board in the 19th century and beyond were very wide-ranging. They included promotion of the arts and sciences underlying industry, protection of industry and commerce by maintaining and enforcing uniform standards of weight and measure, safeguarding against piracy of designs, inventions and trade marks, provision of finance for industry by encouraging and regulating investment in joint stock companies, authorisation of various forms of public utility undertakings, protecting the interests of consumers and traders against monopoly, and improvement of industrial relations.

GOVERNMENT SCHOOLS OF DESIGN

Not all the products of the Industrial Revolution were well-designed or pleasing to look at. According to critics of British manufactures, foreign countries produced goods of better quality and better design possibly because, certainly in

48. 'How Government rewards inventors!' Cartoon from *Fun,* 1866

the cases of France and Germany, there were government schools of design. The brother of Poulett Thomson (President of the Board in 1834 and 1835–39 and later Lord Sydenham) wrote in his *Life of Lord Sydenham* that 'the inferiority of our manufactures in the essential quality of beauty and taste of pattern, to those of the French and some other nations, had long been acknowledged as a great disadvantage in our competition with them, in both the home and foreign market'

Publication of the 1836 report of a Committee investigating the best means of 'extending a knowledge of the arts and of the principles of design among the people (especially the manufacturing population) of the country' and inquiring into the 'constitution, management and effects of institutions connected with the arts' led to Poulett Thomson instituting the School of Design at Somerset House in 1837 as an experiment in the teaching of industrial design. Four provincial schools followed in 1840. The

Board supervised them closely, and by 1849 there were 16, with about 3,000 pupils. 'It would be by their excellence, combined with a moderate price' said one supporter of the schools, himself a manufacturer, 'that British goods would maintain their competitive position.'

A Department of Practical Art was established in 1852 and two years later enlarged to include the Metropolitan School of Science applied to Mining and the Arts, the Museum of Practical Geology, the Geological Survey, the Museum of Irish Industry and the Royal Dublin Society. The Department's name was changed to the Department of Science and Art and it was again expanded to include the London Seamen's School and Nautical School. Through the efforts of Prince Albert, part of the proceeds from the Great Exhibition was spent on land and buildings for a Museum of Manufactures at South Kensington and in 1857 the schools moved there. Their management was then transferred from the Board

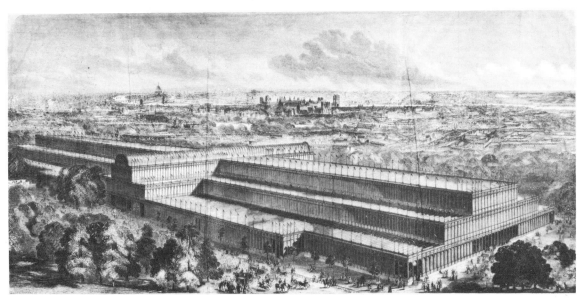

49. View of the Crystal Palace built for the Great Exhibition, 1851.

of Trade to the educational establishment of the Privy Council.

The Great Exhibition of 1851 had celebrated the success of the Industrial Revolution and of UK manufacturers world wide. The Exhibition was sponsored by the Royal family, and a Committee which included the President of the Board of Trade, Henry Labouchere, formed to organise it. Joseph Paxton's Crystal Palace in Hyde Park housed models and drawings of bridge-building, shipbuilding and mining, as well as actual examples of smaller products.

The Boards of Trade and of Education jointly established the British Institute of Industrial Art in 1920. The aim was to 'raise and maintain the standard of modern British industrial art and at the same time to stimulate public appreciation of works of industrial art so as to increase the volume and raise the quality of the demand for these works'. The Institute elected about 100 fellows, including the best known industrial designers, arranged exhibitions at home and abroad, advised government departments and published reports. But lack of finance, after its first two years of Treasury funding, limited its activities. In 1932 a Board of Trade Committee recommended that a central body should be formed, in close association with the Department of Overseas Trade, and that the Board of Trade should be made responsible for the advancement of industrial art in the United Kingdom. In 1934 the Board appointed the Council for Art and Industry as an advisory committee. The present-day Design Council was established by the government in 1944 as the Council of Industrial Design — a grant-aided body sponsored by the Board of Trade to promote improvement of design in British industry. Council members are now appointed by the Secretary of State for Trade and Industry. An Innovation Centre has recently

50.   The Great Exhibition 1851.

37

been set up as an extension to the Design Centre to display new work by designers and inventors.

INDUSTRIES AND MANUFACTURES DEPARTMENT

The Industries and Manufactures department of the Board was set up in 1918 after an inquiry by a departmental Committee into the work and organisation of the Board of Trade. It was a 'new department dealing with home industries, with special reference to their development and stability, production, and the economic strength of the country generally; with questions of policy connected with trade monopolies and combinations, alien penetration into British industries, and the promotion of new trades'.

The new department encouraged industrial research and had a duty to survey the whole field of industrial organisation and to safeguard particular industries by means of tariff protection or import restrictions. Industries then in particular difficulties included shipping, gas, films and cotton. In 1924, on the advice of the then President, Sidney Webb, the government appointed a Committee on industry and trade to inquire into conditions and prospects for British industry with special reference to the export trade, but also with a remit to look into fuel, power and transport facilities, finance and labour conditions, all of which were properly the concern of other government departments. This was at a time of high unemployment and an adverse balance of trade. The Committee produced reports on overseas markets, industrial relations, textile and metal industries, among others.

The country's economic position worsened with the 1930–32 depression, exports declined and competition from foreign imports intensified. The

51. Sidney Webb, President of the Board of Trade, 1924.

change from free trade back to a more protectionist system precipitated the passing of the Import Duties Act 1932 and establishment of the Import Duties Advisory Committee which considered applications for imposition of duties on particular classes of goods. The Merchandise Marks Act 1926 had involved another form of protectionism in giving powers to order compulsory origin marking on certain goods.

The cotton industry was one of the hardest hit. It had experienced almost continuous expansion

for the century before 1914, the great majority of its production being exported overseas. After 1914 the industry declined, with losses in markets where wartime shortages had encouraged development of local industries. Between 1924 and 1938 yarn production had fallen by a third, cloth production had been halved and exports of piece-goods had dwindled by two-thirds. Before World War II, the industry had not been highly concentrated, but had numerous small firms. A joint Committee of cotton trade organisations had helped to prepare the Cotton Industry Reorganisation Act of 1939, but its main principles were put off and the Cotton Industry (Postponement) Act passed. At the start of the war, the cotton industry was still 'unbalanced, unstable, unprofitable and unattractive to labour'. However, two bodies concerned with cotton were set up by an Act of 1940. One, the Cotton Board advised the government on questions related to the industry and maintained and extended exports. When the export drive slackened, the Board administered the financial arrangements of all the cotton concentration schemes and undertook work on behalf of the Board of Trade in connection with export control and utility clothing.

52. Material produced for British Industries Fairs

53. A page from a British Industries Fair catalogue showing prices of the stands, 1915.

One of the tasks of the Board in World War II was to look after home industries and exports. It introduced clothes rationing in 1941 and the Utility Furniture Scheme in 1942, and promoted concentration of industry schemes that enabled workers to be released from civilian industries for war work. Under the Distribution of Industry Act 1945, the Board took general responsibility for development area policy, distribution of industry and resumed its role of adviser on industrial and commercial policy. In 1952 it assumed oversight of the regional boards for industry and, a year later, for industrial productivity.

54. Utility furniture on display at a Board of Trade exhibition at the Building Centre, 1942.

The 1940 report of the Royal Commission on the distribution of the industrial population (the Barlow report) argued that national action was needed to direct the location of industry and so alleviate the problem of concentrated regional unemployment coupled with overcrowded towns and cities. However, during World War II unemployment fell to relatively low levels and the traditional industries of the special areas were kept hard at work. The Ministry of Labour recorded statistics of labour supply while the Board of Trade's Control of Factory and Storage Premises kept a register of buildings and allocated space for industry. In 1940 the Board was working towards contraction of civilian industry to release manpower for the war effort by limiting supplies

55. Board of Trade, Millbank 1940-1952. 'Oliver Lyttelton, when installed here as my predecessor had said "I feel like the last cigar in the box." ' Hugh Dalton: *Memoirs*.

to the home market; raw material allocations were also cut. Production was concentrated into nucleus firms while others closed down for the duration of the war.

Work on post-war policy had already begun in the early 1940s. A department of reconstruction was established within the Board, manned by civil servants and academics. Its task was to consider what to do with wartime controls in the post-war period and one of its objectives was the maintenance of full employment and, as a corollary, regional industrial policy. Hugh Dalton, who was President of the Board in 1942, said that one of his reasons for taking on the job was his wish to do something for depressed areas. He was the only Minister of Cabinet rank who represented a constituency in a depressed area — Bishop Auckland in the North East. The Board's Factory Control had its own regional controllers and staff to find and allocate premises, and its own representatives on each of the regional boards.

In 1942 the Factory Control stressed the need to adapt wartime policies to peacetime needs and recommended retention of licensing of new building so that industrialists looking for factory space would have to come to the Board and so allow officials an opportunity to persuade them to move work to the depressed areas. The government accepted the Board's arguments for controls to be administered in favour of these areas, in its white paper on Employment Policy. This called for government influence over location of new enterprises 'to diversify the industrial composition of areas which are particularly vulnerable to unemployment', removal of obstacles to the transfer of workers from one area to another and from one occupation to another, and provision of training facilities to fit workers for jobs in expanding industries. There were also to be financial incentives for firms wishing to relocate, and building of small new factories by the government.

At each stage the Board of Trade pushed as a priority the steering of industry to the depressed regions during the transition to a peacetime economy. This policy depended on close wartime contacts established between government and industry being continued. The government proposed 'that the channel for the expression of government policy in this matter shall be the Board of Trade, which will be the Department responsible for all general questions of industrial policy and will be suitably strengthened to undertake the heavier responsibilities which the government will assume in this field after the war'.

The Distribution of Industry Act 1945 completed the transfer to the Board of responsibility for regional policy, and for all general questions of industrial policy. It was able to acquire land and erect premises for industry, make loans to firms in development areas and grant or refuse permission to industrialists to build new factories. The Distribution of Industry Act 1950 extended its powers. The improved economic position in the development areas in the late 1940s and early 1950s led to regional policy being given a lower priority in comparison to the export trade, but in 1958 control over industrial development certificates was tightened up, except in development areas where the end of the boom in coal, shipbuilding and steel had caused a consequent sharp increase in unemployment. By the late 1950s, said Sir Frank Lee, Permanent Secretary, the government had succeeded in checking the growth of new industry in some areas and had helped to diversify and strengthen industry in certain development areas – in 1958 there were approximately 1,100 government-owned factories in those regions.

56. Map of the development areas and Northern Ireland, 1955.

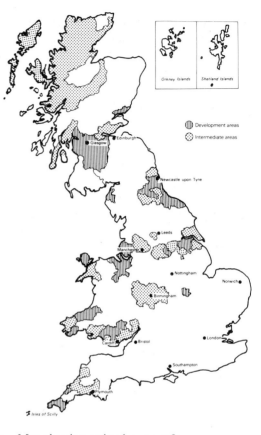

57. Map showing assisted areas, 1984.

The 1960 Local Employment Act repealed the Distribution of Industry Acts, abolished the old development areas and introduced development districts which could be designated by the Board of Trade without the need for Parliamentary approval. It also strengthened the Board's other powers in connection with regional policy. The Labour government of 1964 introduced new powers and gave regional policy matters to the new Department of Economic Affairs. However, the Board continued to offer aid under the Local

Employment Acts by providing factories for rent or sale, and making loans and grants. The industrial development certificate system was strictly enforced and extended to offices. By 1970 the government had developed a wide range of regional aids and assistance and there were intermediate, development and special development areas.

The Department of Trade and Industry now has seven regional offices in England, representing the Department in its dealings with industry, local

42

authorities and other bodies and the regional offices of other government departments. They administer regional development grants and grants from Europe for small firms and export promotion work. The Department is also responsible for the designation of assisted areas and derelict land clearance areas, provision of government-funded offices and factories, European Community regional policy, and other assistance and advice. In 1984 a new regional industrial policy was launched, putting the emphasis on job creation and reducing the bias towards capital-intensive investment. It extended the coverage of the assisted areas map and divided it into two categories, and brought in a new scheme of regional development grants.

58.   The Queen's Award to Industry Scheme, established 1965 to recognise and encourage outstanding achievements in exports and technological innovation.

THE NATIONAL ENTERPRISE BOARD

The Industrial Reorganisation Corporation was set up in 1966, as part of the 'big is beautiful' drive, its special function being 'to search for opportunities to promote rationalisation schemes which could yield substantial benefits to the national economy'. It gave priority to schemes offering good prospects of early returns in terms of increased exports or reduced import requirements, and the Government hoped it would secure a 'lasting improvement in the structure and competitive strength of British industry'.

The white paper *The Regeneration of British Industry* and the Industry Act 1975 led to the founding of the more interventionist National Enterprise Board to build on and enlarge activities previously carried out by the Industrial Reorganisation Corporation. Its chairman and members were appointed by the Secretary of State for Industry, and it was funded by the Department. Its purposes were to develop and assist the UK economy and promote industrial efficiency and international competitiveness; its functions were to establish, maintain or promote industrial undertakings, to promote industrial democracy and take over publicly owned securities or other publicly owned property. By January 1979 the NEB owned BL Ltd, Rolls-Royce (1971), Inmos, Ferranti, ICL, Logica and many other companies. It also sought ways of assisting small firms and regional ventures.

In 1981 NEB merged with the National Research Development Corporation to form the British Technology Group. This is responsible to Parliament through the Secretary of State for Trade and Industry, and it aims to promote the development and commercialisation of technology derived from UK public sector sources such as universities, research councils and establishments and other government bodies. It takes responsibility for protecting and licensing inventions, providing funds and negotiating licensing agreements with industry. But it no longer has the automatic right of first refusal to exploit discoveries, thus creating a more competitive environment.

The Patent Office and its associated Trade Marks and Designs Registries have been part of the Board of Trade since the late 19th century and closely connected with the development of commerce and industry since the Industrial Revolution. Patents give protection for a limited time (now 20 years) to inventions; trade marks are protected against counterfeiting; and the registration of designs which please the eye protects those designs for up to 15 years. The patents system encourages the making of inventions by rewarding the inventor with a monopoly for a limited period. At the same time, the public benefits from information about the invention that must be made available by the inventor in return for the patent. Trade marks enable a trader to differentiate his products from those of others and the consumer benefits by being able to identify the source of goods. The registered design system stimulates the creation of new designs by giving the designer a monopoly.

The earliest known English patent was granted by Henry VI to Flemish-born John of Utynam in 1449 for making stained-glass windows for Eton College and gave him a 20-year monopoly for his method. The word 'patent' derives from the practice of kings in the Middle Ages conferring rights and privileges by means of open letters or *litterae patentes* intended for public view and inspection. But under Elizabeth I and James I the granting of monopolies became subject to abuse. In 1610 James declared that he would only grant patents for 'projects of new invention so they be not contrary to the law nor mischievous to the State'. This was followed by the Statute of Monopolies 1624, which allowed patent monopolies for 14 years for 'any manner of new manufacture' to the 'true and first inventor'.

The Patent Office itself was set up in 1852 under the control of the Commissioners of Patents to act as the country's sole office for the granting of patents of invention. The Designs Registry had existed from 1839 and was transferred to the Patent Office in 1875, while the Trade Marks Registry had come into operation on 1 January 1876 as a result of the passage of the Trade Marks Act 1875.

In 1883 a revised Patent Bill was introduced by Joseph Chamberlain, then President of the Board of Trade. The Bill's main features included a reduction in patent fees from £25 to £5, simplification of procedures, deposit of a complete specification before grant of a patent, and a system of examinations. The granting of patents was to be taken from the Patent Commissioners and assigned to a Comptroller-General of Patents, Designs and Trade Marks, serving under the Board of Trade.

In that year (1883) about 6,000 applications were filed, and in 1884 the figure rose to 17,000 because of the reduction in fees. (In 1982 applications numbered around 33,000.) The building first occupied by the Patent Office had originally been built in 1792 for the 'Masters in Ordinary in Chancery ... and for the Secretaries of Bankrupts and Lunatics ...' The original library where applications and patent publications could be consulted was situated in a long corridor and nicknamed the 'drain pipe'. (Today the principal facilities for providing access to patent information are at the Science Reference Library, developed out of the Patent Office Library.) In August 1944 the whole front of the Office facing Staple Inn was destroyed by a flying bomb, but fortunately the original register was preserved.

59. Patent Office Library 1886.

60. Damage to Patent Office caused by flying bomb, 24 September 1944.

61. A caricature of the original Patent Office Library known as the 'Drain-Pipe'.

62. A patent
for a process,
1886.

Improved Treatment of the Wheat Germ and Broken Wheat.

I, RICHARD SMITH, Flour Mill, Stoke on Trent, in the County of Stafford, Mille
do hereby declare the nature of this invention to be as follows:—

The objects of my invention are:—1st. To act on the wheat germ so as to bring
into a condition more suitable for use as an article of human food; 2nd. To greatl
5 improve the flavor and quality of wheaten flour; and, 3rd. To toughen all parts of th
skin of grains of wheat.

I attain my first object by submitting the germ of wheat to the intimate action u
steam in an enclosed space, by which means such germ is rendered more suitable fo
use in conjunction with flour for the manufacture of bread or other article c
10 human food.

To improve the flavor and quality of wheaten flour I utilize the steam which ha
germ as above described in connection with th

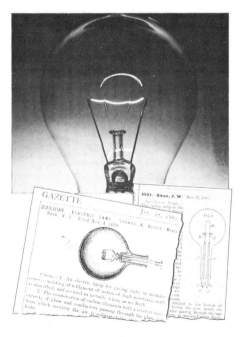

63. The
electric light
bulb patented
almost
simultaneously
by Edison and
Swan on either
side of the
Atlantic.

Bennett Woodcroft FRS (1808–79), first as Superintendent of the Specifications and then later as Clerk to the Commissioners of Patents, initiated the printing of these patent specifications, abstracts and indexes. Shortly before the 1883 Act was passed, a small number of special indexing and abridging clerks were appointed to revise and extend the work done under Woodcroft and these clerks subsequently became the first patent examiners. In 1905, examiners' duties were extended by the introduction of an official search through existing patents to determine whether each alleged invention really was new. The Act of 1949 gave the Comptroller the power to reject an application for lack of novelty. Under the Patents Act 1977, the search by examiners was extended further to investigate whether an invention is obvious or not to a person who is skilled in the relevant field.

Among the inventions patented since the Office was set up are the method of milling used to preserve the wheat germ used in Hovis bread (1886), the jet engine (1930), the patent of the formula for the synthetic fibre 'Terylene' (1946) and – patented almost simultaneously in the USA and UK by Edison and Swan, 1878–79 – the electric light bulb.

The centenary of the Trade Marks Registry was celebrated in 1976. A trade mark is a means of identification enabling traders to make their goods easily recognisable to customers and distinguishable from other traders' goods. It can be a word or emblem or combination of both. However, not all trade marks qualify to be registered and the standards to be met have remained essentially the same since 1876. The mark must be distinctive in itself, non-deceptive and not confusingly similar to any other. Trade marks are of fundamental commercial importance and constantly come to the public attention in

everyday life. Hundreds of thousands of marks
have been registered over the years and have
helped to bring wealth to manufacturers and
merchants, while assisting consumers in their
choice of goods. The demand for the Registry's
services has never been higher. Many registered
marks have become household names, such as
BASS, COLMANS, KODAK, DAZ, KIT KAT and
DULUX: others are immediately recognised for
their visual appeal. So far, the trade mark
registration system has only covered goods. It is
now being extended to cover services such as
banking, insurance, dry cleaning, car repairing,
etc.

The first legislation to protect textile designs
and give some measure of legal ownership was
enacted in 1787. A petition from certain southern-
based textile firms in that year had complained of
losses caused by 'base and mean copies' of their
new patterns, and begged for protection. Piracy
increased as demand for printed textiles grew.
Despite opposition from north-country firms, a
temporary Act was passed giving protection to
designers, printers and owners for two months. It
was renewed in 1789 and made permanent (with
the period extended to three months) in 1794.
Only linen, calico, cotton and muslin were
covered. Two design protection acts were passed
in 1839. The first extended protection to silk, hair
and wool products; the second gave copyright to
metal articles for three years, to others for one
year, and to designs for all articles of manufacture
except lace and those previously provided for. The
Designs Registry was set up in 1839 in response to
growing demands from Britain's textile
manufacturers for statutory protection for their
designs.

However, these Acts still only offered partial
protection. The then President of the Board of
Trade (Poulett Thomson) was MP for

64. Trade marks.

Manchester, and so represented many of those with a vested interest in piracy – an invidious position to be in. His successor, Henry Labouchere, suggested an extension to six months, others held out for a year. At that time the cost of registering a design was one guinea, and the register was open to inspection on payment of five shillings. Well worth it for the pirates, one would think.

A Select Committee set up in 1840 advocated extension to the copyright. In due course the Design Act 1842 was passed and created 13 classes of designs, attempting to cover all manufactured goods, with varying lengths of protection. Two

65. Trade mark submitted for a cotton design.

kinds of registers were kept: one with all the registration details, the other containing the actual samples or paper design.

In 1875 the Board of Trade's jurisdiction over designs was transferred to the Patent Commissioners, and in due course vested in the Patent Office; thus it became a Board concern once more. The largest number of applications for registration today, other than textiles, are for toys, games, containers and electrical and electronic goods. Designs registered in 1983 totalled 6,878. Designs cannot be registered for sculptures, wall plaques, medals or any printed matter, These are all covered by copyright, also a Board of Trade responsibility.

The Patents and Designs Act 1907, which repealed the 1883 Act, made several major changes in the law, including the extension of the term of protection to 15 years by two five-year extension terms. Provision was also made for registration of a design already registered for one class in a second class. Further amending Acts were passed in 1907 and 1932, the latter introducing appeals to an Appeal Tribunal and a system of compulsory licensing. The present Registered Designs Act 1949 abolished the registration of designs by classes and allowed registration in respect of any article or set of articles.

Copyright has played, and continues to play, an important part in the cultural and economic development of the United Kingdom. The protection it affords encourages authors, and enables industries based on their works, to flourish. The first Copyright Act was enacted in 1709 and dealt only with books, but it was soon realised that it did not go far enough to protect authors' interests, and that creators of other kinds of works, such as music or plays, also needed protection. Statutes in the 18th and 19th centuries dealt with copyright in literary works, engravings,

66. Cartoon by Sir David Low against the 'Tuppenny Bill' of April 1928, published in the *Evening Standard.*

music and drama, and fine arts. In 1911 the first real attempt was made to deal comprehensively with copyright in a single Act. It covered literary, musical, dramatic and artistic works already protected by the existing separate statutes, and also recognised the emergence of the gramophone by giving protection against copying to the producers of sound recordings.

The 1911 Act was superseded by the Copyright Act of 1956 which is still in force. New species protected were films and broadcasts. However, since 1956 there has been an explosion in publishing, broadcasting and the music industry, allied with technical developments which greatly facilitate the copying of copyright works. The 1956 Act has been amended to deal with video piracy and to enable cable television and satellite broadcasting. General reform of the law was considered by a Department of Trade Committee under the Hon Mr Justice Whitford, which reported in 1977. A consultative paper on reform of the law relating to copyright, designs and performers' protection was issued in 1981 and a further consultative document published in 1985 on the recording of audio and video copyright material.

The instructions to the Council of Trade in 1660 included a requirement to consider how the manufactures of the kingdom 'may be further improved to their utmost advantage by a just regulation and standard of weight length and breadth that so the private profitt of the tradesmen or merchants may not destroy ye credit of the comodity and thereby render it neglected and unvended abroad, to the great loss and scandall of these our kingdoms'.

But it was not until the passing of the Standards Act 1866 that the custody of the standards was transferred to the Board of Trade.

The Standards department, attached, surprisingly, to the Railway department of the Board, had a duty to provide and maintain standards of weight and measurement, had custody of the imperial and secondary standards and had to verify them at stated intervals, examined weights and measures used in manufacture and for scientific purposes, made general regulations for the guidance of local authorities in performing their duties, examined and tested patterns of weights and measures and held examinations for inspectors.

The year after the transfer to the Board, a Royal Commission was set up to direct and superintend the steps to be taken to ensure and maintain the efficiency of the standards. The Weights and Measures Act 1878, which provided for comparison of the 'parliamentary copies' of the standards with each other every 10 years and with the imperial standards every 20 years, and successive Acts, entrusted the Board with some control over local standards and with the framing and approval of regulations for the guidance of local inspectors. In 1896 the then President, Charles Ritchie, received a deputation of

67. George IV bronze imperial standard bushel, 1824.

68. George IV bronze imperial standard gallon, quart and pint, 1824.

69. Charles Ritchie, President of the Board of Trade 1895–1900.

inspectors and manufacturers who wished to introduce uniformity into the administration of the weights and measures acts by establishing a central authority.

Now the Secretary of State has the responsibility of maintaining primary standards of the yard, pound, metre and kilogramme, and of deciding when and how to determine or redetermine the value of these standards and any authorised copies. He is also required to maintain certain secondary and tertiary standards of weights and measures, and coinage standards of the weight of each authorised coin of the realm. Local standards are kept by local authorities and the Secretary of State prescribes permissible limits

70. Institute of Weights & Measures exhibition, 75th anniversary, June 1969.

of error and may require authorities to provide or replace particular local standards. These must have valid certificates of fitness issued by the Department of Trade and Industry. The statutory responsibilities of local weights and measures authorities have expanded and their enforcement role broadened over the last 15 years. Inspectors have powers to take action in many breaches of consumer legislation, ranging from the giving of short weight to video piracy.

The National Weights and Measures Laboratory is responsible for administering the Weights and Measures Acts 1963, 1976 and 1979 which impose wide-ranging duties on local authorities. Its main functions are concerned with establishing and maintaining standards of mass, length and volume (the trading parameters) on which a national calibration service is based; examining new designs of weighing or measuring equipment to determine its suitability for use for trade and its certification; exercising powers to control sales by quantity of specified goods, including standardisation of package and container sizes. It also maintains a continuing review of the European Community average system of quantity control over packaged goods, scrutiny of industry codes of practice for packers, liaison with the National Metrological Co-ordinating Unit, and review of metrication and unit pricing policies. The Laboratory also checks the amount of froth on beer!

PYX CHAIR

The Pyx chair was used in the first half of the 19th century by successive Lord Chancellors when presiding at the annual trial of the Pyx, a ceremony (still held in a modified form) which dates back to Edward I. The object of the trial was to satisfy the public that the coins issued from the Mint were accurate both in respect of weight and fineness. The Privy Council were summoned to be present at the trial, and the Court met in the Exchequer Office. This office was eventually moved with the standards to Old Palace Yard, together with the Lord Chancellor's chair. The Exchequer Office was abolished in 1866 and the standards placed under Board of Trade control. The then Warden probably sent the chair to the Chief Officer of the Board. It now stands in the Department of Trade and Industry headquarters at 1 Victoria Street.

EMPLOYMENT AND WORKING CONDITIONS

The reconstituted Board of Trade of 1786 came into being at the height of the Industrial Revolution. Successive inventions, such as Hargreaves' spinning jenny, Arkwright's improved water-frame and Crompton's spinning mule made transformation of cotton-spinning from cottage industry to factory possible. But along with the Industrial Revolution came a host of allied problems. The Board was responsible for regulating the social conditions under which work was carried on only in the areas of merchant shipping, docks and railways. It was not directly concerned with conditions of employment in factories and mines, nor the hours of work of women and children, which were Home Office matters.

But in the second half of the 19th century people became increasingly aware of social problems and the need for reliable data on them. Between 1886 and 1916 the Board dealt with certain important aspects of working life. In 1886 it began to collect

71. 'Trial of the Pyx' at the office of the Comptroller-General of the Exchequer, Whitehall, 1854.

72. Pyx chair in DTI headquarters at 1 Victoria Street.

labour statistics. John Burnett, formerly general secretary of the Amalgamated Society of Engineers and member of the Parliamentary Committee of the TUC, was appointed Labour Correspondent of the Board, and in 1893 a special Labour department was set up within the Board's Commercial and Statistical department after the House of Commons adopted a resolution that 'full and accurate labour statistics should forthwith be collected and published'. Hubert Llewellyn Smith was appointed the first Labour Commissioner. However, the new department was not merely a statistical bureau. It was, said the President, A J Mundella, 'a big thing – larger and more important than the Government itself apprehends. It will do great work in the future.'

The Labour department looked into the causes and extent of unemployment – then, as now, a national problem – and the degree to which manpower resources were being wasted. Figures were kept on strikes and lock-outs, trade unions, and the state of the labour market. As well, an initial attempt at a census of wages was carried out. The first *Annual abstract of labour statistics* was issued in 1894, and a monthly journal, the *Labour Gazette*, began in May 1893. This was a journal for

73. Sir Hubert Llewellyn Smith, first Labour Commissioner, 1893 ; Permanent Secretary 1907–1919.

74. A J Mundella, President of the Board of Trade 1892–94.

the use of workmen and all others interested in obtaining prompt and accurate information on matters specifically affecting labour. Writing in the introduction to that first issue, Llewellyn Smith said 'With mere questions of opinion, the *Labour Gazette* will not be concerned. The aim of the department … is to provide a sound basis for the formation of opinions and not to supply opinions.'

The *Gazette* included returns of immigration and emigration, details of the chief labour disputes and changes in rates of wages and hours of work, and a record of industrial accidents at home and at sea. *Cost of living of the working classes: report of an enquiry by the Board of Trade into working-class rents and retail prices, together with the rates of wages in certain occupations in industrial towns of the United Kingdom in 1912*, the sequel to a similar

inquiry in 1905, was a massive report, issued as a command paper and produced by the department. It included data on retail prices paid for specific items of food and coal, and rates of wages in the building, engineering and printing trades in 93 of the principal towns in the United Kingdom.

Towards the end of the 19th century, despite having no statutory authority to do so, the Board intervened in various trade disputes, notably those in the coal, and boot and shoe trades, mainly

75. A page from the 1912 report on *Cost of living of the working classes.*

76. Churchill and Lloyd George's triumphal balancing act at the expense of their Prime Minister, Asquith, December 1909.

because of the damage caused to industry. The 1896 Conciliation Act was passed to give the Board the necessary authority to negotiate settlement of trade disputes. In 1911 the arbitration and conciliation work was transferred to a Chief Industrial Commissioner and Council, which exercised the existing powers of the Board.

The influence wielded by Winston Churchill (President of the Board of Trade from 1908 to 1910) should not be underestimated. He was President for less than two years but, as Robert Rhodes James has said, he 'flung himself into the cause of social reform with characteristic ardour and determination, and his achievements were considerable'. One of the chief advocates of labour exchanges and unemployment insurance as the pivots of government policy for the unemployed was William (later Lord) Beveridge. He was introduced to Churchill by Beatrice and

77.   The new Labour Exchange, Camberwell Green, 1910.

78.   (far left) Max Beerbohm's celebrated cartoon of Churchill, with his officials at the Board of Trade: 'Oh, I *understand* all these figures, right enough. What we've got to do, gentlemen, is to put some—er—*humanising ginger* into 'em'.

79.   The young William Beveridge.

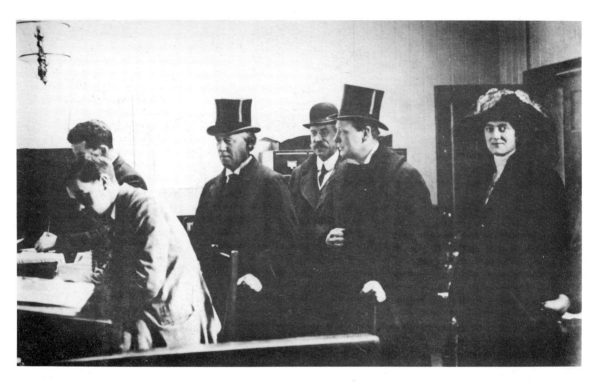

80.
Winston and
Clementine
Churchill with
the Prime
Minister, Mr
Asquith,
during a tour
of newly
opened Labour
Exchanges,
February 1910.

Sidney Webb who advised 'If you are going to deal with unemployment, you must have the boy Beveridge'. He impressed Churchill with his ideas and within his first month at the Board of Trade had drafted a long memorandum on labour exchanges which was incorporated in Churchill's Cabinet paper of 1908 on unemployment insurance and labour exchanges. A network of labour exchanges was set up by the Board under the Act of 1909, primarily to help people find employment, but subsequently to serve as the basis for the work of the 1913 unemployment insurance scheme which was administered by the Board through the exchanges under the National Insurance Act 1911. Churchill reorganised the Labour department into three sections: one to deal with wages, arbitration, conciliation and the

Trade Boards Act; one to deal with statistics, the Census of Production and the *Labour Gazette*; the third with labour exchanges and unemployment.

The combination of labour exchanges and unemployment insurance was intended to be a solution to the unemployment problem and a step towards rational organisation of the labour market. Beveridge and Llewellyn Smith worked together to provide incentives with the national insurance scheme to encourage employers to use the exchanges as a central pool for their casual labour. Provisions in the 1911 Act allowed employers to reach agreement with the Board and make a voluntary arrangement to hire all their casual labour through their local exchanges in return for a reduction in their financial liability for contributions.

THE STAMP
THAT WANTS
A LOT OF
LICKING

AND THE MAN

81. *(above)* 'Here is this great National Insurance Scheme which touches every household, every industry, every trade and all our interests.'

82. *(right)* Lloyd George pushed through the National Insurance Act 1911.

At the turn of the century, the Labour department also campaigned for the reform of trade union law. Since the Trades Union Act 1871 the unions had been regarded as exempt from being sued or having injunctions made against them. The Taff Vale case of 1901 interpreted the law to the contrary, and the unions were up in arms against the judgment. Officials of the Board recommended that existing legislation relating to trade disputes and trade combinations be clarified to allow a fairer treatment of *bona fide* union activities in law. These views were instrumental in the appointment of a Royal Commission to investigate the law on the conduct of industrial relations and were reflected in the Trade Disputes Act 1906.

Another piece of social legislation relating to workers and the Board of Trade was the constitution of machinery under the Trade Boards Act 1909 for the compulsory fixing of minimum wages in what were known as 'sweated' trades. Trades to which the Act originally applied included tailoring, paper box making, machine lace finishing and chain making.

In January 1917 the newly formed Ministry of Labour took over the administration of the Conciliation Act 1896, Trade Boards Act, Labour Exchanges Act, National Insurance (Unemployment) Acts 1911–16, the collection of labour statistics and publication of the *Labour Gazette* (now the *Employment Gazette*).

AN INGENIOUS CONNECTING ROD.

(Not a missing link.)

83.   The Board of Trade mediated in the 1907–1908 dispute between employers in the shipbuilding industry and shipyard workers. Lloyd George met both sides and towards the end of 1908 a settlement was reached. The North-East strikers accepted a wage cut and a conference was to be held to consider setting up a permanent disputes procedure. This was an early example of Board of Trade work on conciliation.

Films

The Department of Trade and Industry, and before that, the Board of Trade, sponsors the British film industry. The Department holds a record of films registered for exhibition purposes going back to 1928. The screen quota for British and foreign-made films started in 1927 as a way of ensuring that a set proportion of British films were shown at cinemas; this system was suspended early in 1983. The Eady Levy (a tax on box office receipts) was introduced in 1949, when Harold Wilson was President, initially as a voluntary measure by exhibitors, and was made a statutory requirement in 1957. This extra income was of vital importance to British film makers as well as being an incentive to investors in indigenous productions and encouraged American film companies to use British facilities and services so that their films would qualify for the Levy.

The National Film Finance Corporation was established in 1949 to encourage a higher level of film production with the aid of government funds. In its first 15 years the NFFC invested in 658 films, in its second 15 years there were only 94, due to a decline in the level of support and of funds. As revenue at the box office dwindled, so did the value of the Eady Levy.

Under the Films Act 1985 the Eady Levy has been abolished, the film quota system removed and the NFFC has been dissolved. Its successor, the British Screen Finance Consortium, is part-funded by government; the Secretary of State can give financial aid for British film production. Assistance is also given to support film project development and the production of short films.

Research establishments

Laboratory of the Government Chemist
The Laboratory's origins can be traced back to 1842 when the Board of Excise established a chemical laboratory to control the operations of

84. A still from 'Gregory's Girl', part-financed by the National Film Finance Corporation.

85. Laboratory of the Government Chemist. Analysis of fibre content of fabrics.

tobacco manufacturers. A second laboratory was set up later to undertake analysis of goods liable to import duty. The two were amalgamated in 1894 and by the early 20th century were carrying out work for several government departments. In 1911 the Laboratory became a separate entity known as the Department of the Government Chemist.

It transferred to DSIR in 1959 and is currently a research establishment of the Department of Trade and Industry. The changes in its work over the years followed the development of analytical chemistry in the UK and requests by successive governments to consider specific problems. Now the Laboratory provides consultancy advice and studies based on chemistry, for both the public and private sectors. It carries out co-operative research and development programmes with industry and manages the DTI's biotechnology support programme.

Tasks carried out in former years included investigations into lead in glazes used for domestic pottery, the use of phosphorus in the Victorian match industry, analysis of the supplies for Captain Scott's 1901 Antarctic Expedition, and the exposure of the Piltdown Man forgery. Recent research work has been on dental cements for fillings, surgical splint bandage material, the application of small-scale robots to laboratory work, and document examination.

National Engineering Laboratory

The National Engineering Laboratory was established in 1947 in order to conduct research and development in a variety of areas in mechanical engineering science. Now the emphasis has shifted to applied research, design, development and testing for specific customers, including government departments and individual organisations and companies. Through the

86. National Engineering Laboratory. Seismic qualification of control on the NEL 20 tonne shaker table.

Department of Trade and Industry's requirements boards, work is funded on a longer-term and broader basis. Research, development, design, consultancy and testing facilities are provided in, for example, microprocessor applications, new forming and fabricating processes, manufacturing technology, and robotics.

National Physical Laboratory

A Committee reported in favour of the establishment of a National Physical Laboratory in 1898. Its purpose was to test and verify instruments for physical investigation, for construction and preservation of standards of measurement, and for the systematic determination of physical constants and numerical data useful for scientific and industrial purposes. The Permanent Secretary of the Board of Trade was an *ex-officio* member of its governing body.

The Laboratory opened officially in 1902 at Bushy Park, Teddington, and among its tasks were investigations carried out for the Board's Standards department. Under the Weights and

Measures Act 1889 the Board had power to make
such 'new denominations of standards for the
measurement of electricity, temperature, pressure
or gravities as may appear to them to be required
for use for trade to be made and duly verified'.

Today the National Physical Laboratory is the
UK's national standards laboratory, its main
function being to provide the metrological infra-
structure. It establishes and maintains a consistent
national measurement system based on national
measurement standards, undertakes research and
international metrological comparisons and
provides laboratory accreditation and consultancy
services. It runs a number of special services such
as the British Calibration Service, Materials
Services Centre, and National Corrosion Service.

Warren Spring Laboratory
Warren Spring was established by the DSIR in
1959. It undertakes sponsored research for
government and industry, dealing with industrial

process technology and environmental pollution;
providing advice, consultancy and facilities on
bulk materials handling technology for powders,
pastes and slurries; materials recovery from
industry, commercial and domestic wastes; air
and oil pollution measurement; and abatement
processes for industry, and national and local
government. Basic applied research is funded by
the Department of Trade and Industry.

British Marine Technology Ltd

The National Maritime Institute provided a range of services to industry and government in fluid dynamics and the associated fields of structural and computational analysis. In 1903 experimental aerodynamics was started in the National Physical Laboratory's engineering department. World War II activities included air-sea rescue, barrage balloons, midget submarines and bouncing bombs. In the 1970s the Institute was formed from the National Physical Laboratory's ship and maritime science divisions. Its work from then on included sea-keeping experiments on high speed craft, the Dover Strait traffic survey, liferaft tests in wind and waves for the Small Craft Committee, and offshore work for the petroleum and gas industries. In 1982 the Institute was privatised and became a private limited company, subsequently British Marine Technology Ltd.

Computer Aided Design Centre

This was established early in 1969 by the Ministry of Technology as the primary UK centre for research, development and application of CAD techniques, and to disseminate information on developments and assist industry to make use of them. It has a specialised consultancy service and supporting software services, and carries out research on graphics, language processing and database technology. CadCentre Ltd was set up in 1983 by a consortium of companies to acquire the business and assets of CADC. As part of the negotiated purchase of the business, transitional arrangements were made with the Department of Trade and Industry to assist the company for the first three years of trading after privatisation.

90. Board of Trade 1814: the Whitehall frontage.

The Board of Trade and Merchant Shipping

GOVERNMENT intervention in the mercantile marine goes back long before the Industrial Revolution. By the early 19th century various government departments were responsible for regulations concerned with shipping. These included the Admiralty (for supply of seamen), the Treasury (for customs) and the Colonial Office and Emigration Commissioners (for passengers).

'Ah! the pigtailed, quidding pirates and
    the pretty pranks we played,
All have since been put a stop-to by the
    naughty Board of Trade;
The schooners and the merry crews are
    laid away to rest,
A little south the sunset in the Islands of
    the Blest.'
    John Masefield: *A Ballad of John Silver*

Merchant shipping has encompassed a mass of detailed regulations over the years – on cargo, ship construction, safety, welfare of seamen, coastguard, oil pollution, shipwreck and salvage, harbours and lighthouses. In fact, successive governments, despite being committed to a *laissez faire* policy, were nevertheless forced to intervene in nearly every aspect of the industry during the 19th century and into the 20th, to ensure safety at sea.

The repeal of the navigation laws in 1848 did away with control of the commercial side of Britain's seaborne trade. But at almost the same time a spate of legislation regulating the merchant fleet sprang up, in the face of fierce opposition from shipowners. President Henry Labouchere, answering a query in 1848 from the Select Committee on Miscellaneous Expenditure about the handling of mercantile questions, said that he

'proposed to establish a department of Mercantile Marine, composed of unpaid officers, of which the members shall be the President and Vice-President of the Board of Trade, one of the Naval Lords of the Admiralty ...one or two persons connected with the merchant navy ...a Board of that description would be most valuable in dealing with all questions that relate to the mercantile marine of the country. The want of it is very much felt'.

91. Henry Labouchere (later Baron Taunton). President of the Board of Trade 1839–1841, 1847–1852.

The Mercantile Marine Act 1850 laid down that 'the "Board of Trade" shall undertake the general superintendence of matters relating to the British mercantile marine...' The Board was to appoint local marine boards at principal ports, register seamen and be responsible for them and for the seamen's fund, and examine masters and mates. The 1854 Merchant Shipping Act consolidated all previous legislation.

In 1857 the then President, Lord Stanley of Alderley, proposed to the Treasury that the whole Board should be revised and reorganised. The reason was, he said, that 'within four years between 1853 and 1857 the business of the Board of Trade had increased nearly threefold; and the number of papers received and despatched had risen from 34,435 in the former year to 93,758 in the latter. During the same brief period the number of persons of all classes required, which by the Committee of 1853 was estimated at *twenty six*, had increased to *sixty four*, besides staff officers. The unavoidable necessity for this was attested by the fact that between 1853 and 1857 successive Acts of Parliament had devolved on the Department no less than twelve entirely new divisions of executive labour, connected with

92. The Port of London Authority was set up in 1908 under Board of Trade control.

Marine affairs, meteorology, pilotage, wrecks, lights and the wages and effects of seamen. Since then further additions have taken place, and others may still be expected.'

In the latter part of the 19th century, the UK merchant fleet became generally dominant, and was still expanding up to 1914. The British economy was holding its own in this area despite the industrialisation of other states. But the demands of a wartime economy finally required a specialised department, and in December 1916 the Ministry of Shipping took over control of sea transport and cargo ship construction. This was related to the replacement of Asquith as Prime Minister by Lloyd George: the new administration also set up Ministries of Labour and of Food in December 1916. The government was more interventionist than hitherto and included some Labour Party ministers. The Ministry of Transport was established in 1919 and took over the Marine department, while the Board's Harbour department was wound up.

Marine department work returned to the Board in 1921 to a renamed Mercantile Marine department. In 1921 the Admiralty's Transport department was transferred to the Board; its duties included the arrangement for conveyance by sea of personnel and stores for government departments. It also prepared – in peacetime – war plans for shipping. In the 1920s and 1930s the department administered the Merchant Shipping Acts, the Coastguard Act 1925 and the tramp shipping subsidy acts.

The post-war boom and freight rates both collapsed around 1921. More fleets were competing for the available business and the years of depression saw progressive deterioration of the condition of the industry, especially in the tramp, or cargo vessel, section. Fierce competition brought down freight charges to unprofitable

93. Ops room. Stan Holness and Sybil Hill.

94. Within hours of the Argentine invasion of the 'Falklands, Shipping Policy Division was setting-up the most massive call-up of merchant ships seen since the Suez operations, in support of the task force. Picture shows the Ops Room; Left to right: Lt. Cdr. Paddy Donovan, John Maccoy, Dick Dymond, Geoff Beilby (standing), Jack Haigh, Capt. Derek Sims and Rodney Start.

levels and, to remedy this as far as possible, the government brought in the British Shipping Assistance Act 1935. This provided for subsidy payments to owners of British tramp ships in respect of voyages made in 1935 (subsequently extended to 1937). The Act laid down that the industry could obtain a grant of loans up to a maximum of £10 million for construction of British ships for British owners, on condition that for each ton built two tons were demolished (ie a 'scrap and build scheme'). This was aimed mainly at helping shipbuilders in Scotland and the North East, who were located in regions of high unemployment.

World War II saw the transfer of the Mercantile Marine in turn to a separate Ministry of Shipping, then to the Ministry of War Transport and afterwards to the Ministry of Transport. A huge wartime burden fell once more on the Merchant Navy, the whole UK fleet was requisitioned, and losses at sea were very heavy (11 million gross tons of shipping). But by the end of 1948 when the main sales of US government ships and distribution of ex-enemy ships as reparations had taken place, the UK fleet was back to its pre-

war strength in terms of tonnage, if not of quality.

In the mid-1960s marine, shipping policy and civil aviation matters were transferred to the Board of Trade. The six-week seamen's strike of 1966, mainly over the pay of ratings, led to the setting-up of two major inquiries which resulted in two notable reports: *The final report of the Court of Inquiry into Certain Matters concerning the Shipping Industry* (the Pearson report) and the *Report of the Committee of Inquiry into Shipping* (the Rochdale report). The Pearson recommendations resulted in the Merchant Shipping Act 1970 – an enabling measure. The report inquired into the trade dispute between shipowners and union, and into the terms and conditions of seamen. It made recommendations on the statutory control of seafarers' conditions of employment, their welfare and the role of the Board of Trade in enforcing marine safety requirements. The Rochdale report reviewed the organisation and structure of the UK shipping industry, its methods of operation and any other factors which might affect its efficiency and competitiveness.

Over a decade later, in Spring 1982, the Department of Trade was responsible for the chartering and requisitioning of the merchant fleet that sailed to the Falklands, carrying troops and supplies.

96. Launch of the *Great Britain* at Bristol, 1843.

SAIL AND STEAMSHIPS

In 1890 sailing ships still made up 40 per cent of the total numbers of the UK merchant fleet, although only 25 per cent by tonnage. Steamships were faster, and independent of wind conditions, but they were used mainly as tugs and for short trips until the paddle wheel was replaced by an efficient propeller and engines made smaller and more economical. Many vessels had sails *and* steam engines at this period. Up to the 1890s Britain had a far higher percentage of vessels powered by steam than her competitors, but this advantage dwindled after 1900. Steamships carried low bulk, high value cargoes like passengers and mail – comparable to present-day aeroplanes.

By the mid-19th century Britain had the resources and technology to become the principal world producer and exporter of iron and coal, and the means to build bigger ships to export this cargo. In 1843 Brunel's iron-hulled ship, the *Great Britain* was launched from Bristol Dock; it had another new feature – its screw propeller. A decade later a Scottish shipbuilder patented a compound marine engine which, by using steam at higher pressure, reduced the amount of fuel required. Steamships could then carry large amounts of cargo economically across the world, and in 1869 the Suez Canal opened up even faster routes.

Board of Trade interest in any ship began at the building stage when it was measured for tonnage before registration. Passenger ships were surveyed by the Board, cargo ships given load-line certificates, officers examined and certificated, crew engaged and discharged in the presence of the Mercantile Marine Office superintendent. The authorities aimed to ensure that ships' officers were competent and, as well, that crews were not

95. Engraving c.1830 which gives vent to public fears of travelling by steamship.

Travelling by Steam!

ill-treated. After the voyage the ship's papers were sent to the Registrar of Shipping and Seamen who was responsible to the Board of Trade.

TONNAGE MEASUREMENT AND SURVEY OF SHIPS

A ship's tonnage was the measurement of its carrying capacity or burden. In the 15th century a ton denoted the space occupied by a tun cask of wine; later, for the purpose of registered tonnage, the space of 100 cubic feet. Government taxation of ship or cargo was based on the ship's tonnage as were lighthouses, pilotage or harbour dues and fees. It was, therefore, to the advantage of shipowners to register their ships at as low a tonnage as possible; they could do this because the rules of measurement were complicated and left several loopholes. The Merchant Shipping Act

1854 contained a practical method of internal measurement devised by Mr G Moorsom, who was appointed Surveyor General of Tonnage the following year. Another personage who had some lasting influence on unseaworthy ships was the MP for Derby, Samuel Plimsoll (1824–98, the 'sailors' friend') who had entered Parliament in 1868. He opened his campaign for improving the safety of ships in 1870. His idea of a fixed load-line was rejected by the 1873 Royal Commission, but in 1874 his Bill to impose the line was defeated by only three votes. The campaign reached its climax in 1875 when Plimsoll made a scene in the Commons, violently attacking the shipowners and

97. Gauging wine casks, London Docks, 1900. A ship's tonnage was the measurement of its carrying capacity; in the 15th century a ton denoted the space occupied by a tun cask of wine.

98. Samuel Plimsoll MP (1824–1898). The 'Sailors' friend'

67

refusing to withdraw. He was sent out by the Speaker, but the incident excited public interest and the government hurried through the 1876 Merchant Shipping Act, in which the Plimsoll line was introduced. This was a marking on the hull of all cargo vessels showing the safe levels to which the ship could be loaded. Through subsequent legislation in 1890, the Board of Trade was empowered to determine how the load-line should be marked, and in 1906 British requirements as to load-line and seaworthiness were applied to foreign ships using British ports.

The professional aspects of Marine division's work are now carried out by the Marine Survey Service, headed by the Surveyor General of Ships for the United Kingdom. The staff ensure that ships registered in the UK (and certain others) conform to structural, manning and lifesaving equipment requirements appropriate to their class. The service is also responsible for the survey of all UK merchant ships for tonnage and load-line, the hull survey of UK passenger ships and survey work on cargo ships. It carries out research, especially on the carriage of dangerous goods, craft and installations used by the offshore industry, and the safety of fishing vessels.

The Marine division and its work was transferred to the Department of Transport in 1983.

99.   Recruiting for the Navy, Tower Hill 1859.

100.   The Press Gang, by 'Phiz'.

WORKING CONDITIONS

After 1792, with the Navy engaged in the Napoleonic wars, the hunger for crew was almost insatiable. Men were seized from merchant ships and from dry land, and agents known as 'crimps' illegally impressed or kidnapped men for service at sea. In the early years of the 19th century seamen led a life of danger and hardship, often on unseaworthy ships. There were no national unions, and the State seldom intervened to ensure their welfare.

CAUTION.

CRIMPING.

At the Thames Police Court, London, on the 17th October, 1901, a boarding-house keeper was convicted of having unlawfully demanded and received from four Seamen who had been staying at his house, remuneration for providing them with employment on board ship, in contravention of Section 112 of the Merchant Shipping Act, 1894, and was fined

£8 and THIRTEEN GUINEAS COSTS,

MAKING IN ALL

£21 13s. 0d.

or in default of immediate payment imprisonment.

The above-mentioned Section provides a penalty not exceeding five pounds for demanding or receiving directly or indirectly any remuneration whatever for providing a Seaman or Apprentice with employment.

WALTER J. HOWELL,
ASSISTANT SECRETARY
MARINE DEPARTMENT

BOARD OF TRADE

CAUTION.

SCURVY.

At the Police Court, Newcastle-upon-Tyne, on the 13th January, 1903, a Shipmaster was convicted of having failed to provide a sufficient quantity of Lime Juice, as required by Section 200 and the 5th Schedule of the Merchant Shipping Act, 1894, and was fined

£10 and COSTS amounting to £15 0s. 7d.

The same Shipmaster was convicted of having failed to make entries in the Official Logbook with reference to the illness of two Seamen, as required by Sections 240 and 241 of the Merchant Shipping Act, 1894, and was fined

£5 and

MARINE DEPARTMENT
BOARD

NOTICE

TO

SHIPOWNERS & MASTERS.

YELLOW FEVER AT RIO.

The Board of Trade have received from Her Majesty's Consul at Rio de Janeiro, a Report upon the subject of the epidemic of Yellow Fever at that port in the year 1878.

The epidemic, which commenced in December, 1877, increased in intensity up to February, 1878, and did not abate until the end of the following month. It thus appears that the months of January, February, and March are those which are most unhealthy at the Port.

It further appears from the Returns which accompany the Report, that the death rate from Yellow Fever is much higher in the case of those persons who were not submitted to medical treatment upon the first manifestation of the symptoms.

The Board of Trade desire, therefore, to impress upon Masters the urgent necessity for at once sending to the Hospital any Seamen showing symptoms of Yellow Fever, instead of waiting until the disease has gained ground, and by its progress has rendered ineffectual any remedies which may then be applied.

THOMAS GRAY,

By Order of the Board of Trade, Assistant Secretary,
December, 1879. Marine Department.

Handbill No. 24. F & T 3000 12–79 M 16,920
1879.

The Merchant Seamen's Act 1835 aimed to remedy this state of affairs, saying that the 'prosperity, strength and safety [of the kingdom] principally depend on a large, constant and ready supply of seamen … it is necessary to aid by all practicable means, the increase of the number of such seamen, and to give them all due encouragement and protection'. Between 1830 and 1860 the Board played an increasing part in introducing legislation aimed at protecting the rights of seamen. By 1850 it was generally responsible for the welfare of the country's mariners, including conditions at sea for officers and men, discipline, the prevention of crimping (the procurement or impressment of seamen), the engagement, discharge and payment of seamen, supply of medicine and medicaments such as lime

69

juice to prevent scurvy, and the registry of seamen.

Others were concerned about what happened to the seamen aboard ship. In 1843 and again four years later, James Murray, a civil servant at the Foreign Office had written to British consuls overseas asking about the conditions of British shipping in local ports. These reports, nearly all unfavourable, were presented to Parliament in 1848. The Board's president, Henry Labouchere, said that he hoped the evidence would convince shipowners that it was to their advantage for the government to act quickly to remedy the bad conditions. The Board of Trade, said James Murray when advocating the establishment of a Board of Commercial Marine, was the logical office for such a department as it seemed 'the office to which the mercantile community naturally look in regard to everything relating to trade, whether on shore or at sea'.

There are now extensive regulations relating to discipline and desertion, payment of wages and standards of accommodation for crew. The marine offices are focal points for assistance on a wide range of matters, such as casualty investigations and death inquiries, crew welfare and documentation.

METEOROLOGY

Before 1830 the weather, as it affected ships and sailing, received little attention. But with increased competition among shipowners, the use of ships in winter and worries about safety at sea,

SAVE YOUR WAGES.

When you come back to port after a long voyage and have to receive wages amounting to three pounds or more, it is a pity, and it is your own fault, if you and your wife, children, mother, or sister, or whoever may be keeping your home together, do not have the use of the money.

If you stop in a strange port, you may get into debt, lose your well-earned money, get disease into the bargain, and you will have to rely on an advance before you can go to sea again.

If you make haste to your own home, and have your money sent after you, you will not have to get into debt in a strange place, you will not lose your money, and you will save your health. But more than all this, you, and those you desire to help, will be gainers with you, and you will save your clothes, and not need an advance next voyage.

Therefore, when you arrive in port at the end of this voyage ask the Board of Trade Officer, as soon as he boards your ship, to arrange for your passage home to your family at once, and to send your wages after you. He will give you a paper to fill up, a Railway warrant for yourself, some cash for the journey, and will see you off.

Do not hesitate, but go at once; have your money home, save your clothes, save your health; spend your money amongst the friends of your home; help those at home who are anxiously expecting you.

THOMAS GRAY.

Board of Trade,
March 1885.   (P.T.O.

Handbill No. 25.
1. 18216. 10,000—2 85.   Wt. 21673.—E. & S.

102. The welfare of seamen was a prime consideration of the Marine department of the Board of Trade.

103. Vice-Admiral Robert Fitzroy, CB, FRS. First head of the Meteorological department.

interest grew in the study of meteorology and hydrography. The Hydrographic Office of the Admiralty was set up in 1795 and carried out surveys of coasts in many parts of the world. It published its first official catalogue of naval charts in 1830 and, two years later, the first official tide tables. At the beginning of 1855 the Board of Trade created a Meteorological department headed by Captain (later Admiral) Robert Fitzroy, ex-commander of the *Beagle*, who had carried out the survey of the Patagonian coasts and the Straits of Magellan, to which Charles Darwin had been attached in the 1830s. The primary duty of the new department was to collect observations on weather and ocean currents for use by shipping.

The Board had no authority but acted as liaison between the Meteorological Office and merchant ships. It paid half of Fitzroy's salary of £600, and the Admiralty the other half. Fitzroy instituted the system of storm warnings which subsequently developed into the present system of daily forecasts for shipping. The Board of Trade encouraged shipowners to buy and install the necessary equipment of barometer, hydrometers, thermometers and azimuth compass, and delegated agents to teach shipmasters how to use them and keep proper logs. From 1867 a Committee of the Royal Society took over control of the Meteorological Office, at the request of the government.

LIGHTHOUSES AND PILOTAGE

By 1835 there were over 200 lighthouses around the British Isles, operated or controlled by those owning or leasing the land on which they were built. As the amount of dues charged to ships

passing the light was usually set by the owners, these were highly profitable investments. But by the early 19th century three bodies had control of half the lighthouses – Trinity House of Deptford, the Ballast Board of Dublin and, in Scotland, the Commissioners of Northern Lights.

With an increasing number of shipwrecks, demand for reform and the lowering of duties grew. In 1822 a select Committee of the House of Commons advised that all lighthouses should be

104. The Board of Trade became responsible for lighthouses in 1853.

put under the control of Trinity House, but this was not implemented. Another Committee in 1834 recommended again that they should be put under one board; its chairman, Joseph Hume, introduced a Bill in 1835 and in the following year demanding that lighthouses be supervised by the Board of Trade, for 'what was the Board of Trade for, if not to undertake the management of such matters as this?' He was persuaded to withdraw his Bill and the President of the Board, Poulett Thomson, presented a government Bill giving control of lighthouses in England and Wales to Trinity House, with tacit supervision by government via the already close relations established between the Board and Trinity House. The lighthouses were financed by dues levied on ships using UK ports. Trinity House bought out the private lights in 1836, helped by a government loan. In 1853 supervision of lighthouse authorities and the mercantile marine fund was given to the Board of Trade. The Board had powers to make pilotage orders regulating pilotage in particular districts, ships' lights and fog signals. The Harbour department of the Board, created in 1867, was put in charge of foreshores, administration of pilotage and lighthouses, and management of certain lighthouses overseas.

SHIPWRECKS

Safety of life at sea had been a Board of Trade concern since the beginning of the 19th century. After the Napoleonic wars the merchant fleet had suffered neglect, and owners had been keener on making quick profits than on looking after their ships. With increasing competition from abroad, mainly from American-owned ships, wrecks were frequent and passengers and crew suffered from bad accommodation, insufficient food and water.

In the three years leading up to 1835, 1,702 UK ships and 2,682 lives were lost. In 1836 a Select Committee on shipwrecks reported. Its remit was to 'inquire into the causes of the increased number of shipwrecks, with a view to ascertain whether such improvements might not be made in the construction, equipment and navigation of merchant vessels, as would greatly diminish the annual loss of life and property at sea'. The Committee found that losses were due in large measure to the defective construction of ships, their bad state of repair, improper or excess loading, incompetent masters and mates, drunkenness – in fact almost all kinds of inadequacy and incompetence. It recommended the formation of a Mercantile Marine Board. A Bill to this effect was introduced by James Silk Buckingham in early 1837 which provided for the establishment of a Marine Board to direct and regulate the UK mercantile marine; it was not particularly well received. Poulett Thomson, then President of the Board, argued that one of the reasons for the greatness of the British merchant marine was the lack of government interference, and said that the Bill covered details not susceptible to legislation. He was even more vehement at the second reading saying that the Bill was so faulty in its detail that it would be impossible to carry into law, and a marine board would be too costly and have too much power. Labouchere, then Vice-President of the Board, felt that the Bill represented vexatious interference with the shipping interest of the country and would inflict a great blow upon it. The Bill was voted out.

In 1843 yet another Committee investigated the causes of shipwrecks. It inquired into the loss of British vessels and the means of diminishing that loss in future; also into the means of preserving the lives and property of shipwrecked persons. It confined its recommendations to specific details, but again they were not accepted. The *Westminster Review* in 1844 called the then protected shipping interest 'the nation's spoiled child [which] is come to maturity half instructed and reckless'. A great many maritime disasters, it said, 'must be set down to the sheer default of the shipowner and his servants'. Reforms eventually occurred in piecemeal fashion; for example, with the 1846 Act for the regulation of steam navigation, which granted the Board of Trade the right to inquire into accidents.

Ensuring that masters and mates were competent appeared to be one of the best remedies for unnecessary casualties, and an increasing number of memorials were submitted to the Board requesting examinations. In 1842 Captain Fitzroy headed a deputation to the Board on a proposed measure to establish examination boards in various parts of the country. But it was

CAUTION TO OWNERS AND MASTERS.

Overcrowding on Passenger Steamers.

The Board of Trade desire to call the special attention of Owners and Masters of Passenger Steamers to the danger of overcrowding their vessels, and to warn them of the penalties to which they will render themselves liable if they infringe the provisions of the Merchant Shipping Act, 1894 (Section 283), which are as follows :—

"283. The Owner or Master of any Passenger Steamer shall not receive on board thereof, or on or in any part thereof, any number of Passengers which, having regard to the time, occasion, and circumstances of the case, is greater than the number allowed by the Passenger Steamer's Certificate, and if he does so, he shall for each offence be liable to a Fine not exceeding TWENTY POUNDS, and also to an additional Fine not exceeding FIVE SHILLINGS for every Passenger above the number so allowed, or if the Fare of any Passenger on board exceeds Five Shillings, not exceeding double the amount of the Fares of all the Passengers above the number so allowed, reckoned at the highest rate of fare payable by any Passenger on board."

WALTER J. HOWELL,

Assistant Secretary,

Board of Trade, *Marine Department.*

March, 1900.

Handbill No. 125A.

105. Board of Trade handbill.

106. The after-part of the *Princess Alice* on shore below Woolwich after the collision with the *Bywell Castle*, 1878.

not until 1845 that the Board instituted a system of voluntary examinations with delegated authority for their administration by Trinity House. These were unpopular with owners and officers alike and few bothered to sit for them until regulations laid down that ships chartered by government required qualified masters and mates. The 1850 Act made examination of masters and mates compulsory.

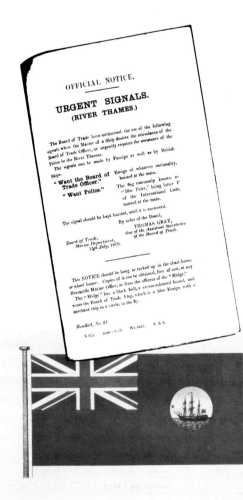

107. Handbill, 1879 and Board of Trade Flag.

Other statutory safety measures that became part of the Board's duties were regulations as to lifesaving apparatus and registration, construction and repair, and navigation rules. The Board was also responsible for shipping on the Thames. Later, Lloyd George's 1906 Merchant Shipping Act was criticised by the Conservatives as quasi-protectionist. It confined pilots' certificates to British subjects and forced foreign ships using British ports to conform to certain UK fleet standards.

The Harbour department of the Board was generally in charge of wreck and salvage under the Merchant Shipping Acts. It appointed Receivers of Wrecks and supervised their work. Under the Merchant Shipping Act 1894 these officials had wide powers to save life and property and protect owners' interests. They also protected the rights of the Crown to the proceeds of unclaimed wrecks, and laid down procedures for settling disputes over salvage. The Board received reports on all casualties and decided whether they should be the subject of a formal inquiry held by a Court, or by a Wreck Commissioner or Inspector. An Act was passed in 1973 to protect historic wrecks in territorial waters, and the sites of such wrecks from interference by unauthorised persons. The *Mary Rose* is probably the best known shipwreck that has benefited from this Act in recent years.

TITANIC

On 14–15 April 1912 the British passenger liner *Titanic* hit an iceberg south east of Newfoundland on her maiden voyage and sank within three hours. Less than a third of her passengers (711 out of 2,201) survived. A formal investigation was set up by the Board of Trade, with Lord Mersey as Wreck Commissioner and five assessors. The Commission recommended that foreign-going passenger and emigrant steamships should in future have watertight subdivision of bulkheads, watertight decks, provision of lifeboats and rafts, based on the number of passengers, and that 'Board of Trade inspection of boats and life-saving appliances should be of a more searching character than hitherto'.

108. The last message received from the *Titanic* after she struck an iceberg in mid-Atlantic, 1912.

SHOWING THE LINER BREAKING IN TWO: SKETCHES OF THE STAGES OF THE SINKING OF THE "TITANIC" MADE BY MR. JOHN B. THAYER JUN. WHILE HE WAS ON ONE OF THE VESSEL'S COLLAPSIBLE BOATS, AND FILLED IN BY MR. L. P. SKIDMORE, ON THE "CARPATHIA," IMMEDIATELY AFTER THE RESCUE OF THE SURVIVORS.

We publish here, by courtesy of the "New York Herald," remarkable drawings of the end of the "Titanic." They are of very special interest in that they show the stages of the sinking of the liner sketched by Mr. John B. Thayer jun. while he was actually on one of the vessel's overturned collapsible boats after the disaster, and, particularly, inasmuch as they show that the liner broke in two before disappearing beneath the waters. The sketches were filled in by Mr. L. P. Skidmore, of Brooklyn, on the "Carpathia" immediately after the picking up of the survivors from the "Titanic's" boats. It will be noted that Mr. Thayer times and describes his drawings as follows: "11.45 p.m. Strikes starboard bow, 12 feet aft—12.5 a.m. Settles by head. Boats ordered out—1.40 a.m. Settles to forward stack. Breaks between stacks—1.50 a.m. Forward end floats, then sinks—2 a.m. Stern section pivots amidships and swings over spot where forward section sank—Last position in which 'Titanic' stayed five minutes before the final plunge." Mr. Thayer is the son of the second Vice-President of the Pennsylvania Railway. Mr. John B. Thayer sen., who was a victim of the disaster. The latter's wife and her maid were saved.

109. 'Made by a survivor, on an overturned collapsible boat, as the "Titanic" was sinking.' *Illustrated London News*, 11 May 1912.

The United States also held an inquiry, and its Committee on Commerce Report No 806, 1912, recommended that there should be sufficient lifeboats to accommodate every passenger and every crew member, stressed the necessity for regulation of radiotelegraphy, and that additional structural requirements should include watertight bulkheads. Evidence given to the US Committee paints a striking picture of the catastrophe: 'The ship went down gradually by the bow, assuming an almost perpendicular position just before sinking at 12.47 pm New York time ... the preponderance of evidence is to the effect that she assumed an almost end-on position and sank intact'.

The disaster, while an appalling national tragedy, was also traumatic for the Board. It led directly to the calling of the first international conference on the safety of life at sea, which produced multilateral agreement on lifesaving and fire-fighting appliances, on subdivision and fireproofing in passenger ships, and on wireless distress procedures.

BOILER EXPLOSIONS

Increased use of steamships led inevitably to frequent boiler explosions in the early 19th century. Committees in 1817 and 1831 recommended various safety devices, but legislation was put off, as it was again after a

111. Boiler explosion at Barking, Essex. Report no. 1173, 1899.

110. Board of Trade inquiry into the Sinking of the *Titanic*.

further Committee in 1839 investigated the causes of steamboat accidents and said that the Board of Trade should institute a system of periodical survey and should license all steam vessels. Finally, after the 1843 inquiry into the causes of shipwreck, the Board was persuaded to enact a Bill for the regulation of steam navigation, by which it was to survey all steam vessels, their hulls and machinery.

112. Board of Trade handbill.

As part of the Marine department's responsibilities, inquiries were held into boiler explosions, both on land and at sea, under the provisions of the boiler explosions acts. A report was published on each inquiry and an annual return made. The Notice of Accidents Act 1894 laid down that the Board of Trade had to be notified of accidents at work and had power to hold formal investigations, especially in cases of construction or repair of railroads or tramways.

EXPLOSIONS OF COAL GAS ON BOARD SHIP.

Official Caution.

THE attention of Shipowners, Shipmasters, and Underwriters is specially directed to the facts elicited by inquiry into the following cases of explosion of Coal-gas.

"LEVANT," of Liverpool. Official Number, 51,378.

On April 25th 1877, the S.S. "Levant" commenced to take in a cargo of South Wales coal of the description commonly called "Davis's Merthyr Steam Coal." She sailed from Cardiff on the 26th of the same month, bound for Gibraltar, and in consequence of heavy weather the hatches were battened down and were not removed until the 28th. At 6 a.m. on that day the mate gave orders for one hatch to be taken off each hold. This was done, but about three-quarters of an hour afterwards the explosion took place in the forecastle, in consequence of one of the crew igniting a match. A formal investigation into the circumstances attending the casualty was held at Liverpool before T. S. Raffles, Esquire, Stipendiary Magistrate, Captains Grant and Wilson acting as Assessors. The Court were of opinion that the explosion was clearly due to the want of proper ventilation, which caused an accumulation of gas in the forecastle, and considered that vessels carrying cargoes similar to that of the "Levant" should be fitted with efficient deck ventilators. Five men were injured by the explosion.

"SARDINIAN," of Glasgow. Official Number, 71,695.

The "Sardinian" (an iron screw steamer of 2,577 tons register) left Liverpool on May 9th 1878, bound for Quebec, and anchored at Moville, Lough Foyle, where the explosion occurred the following morning. The Court of Inquiry held at Liverpool before the Wreck Commissioner (Commander Forster and Captain Castle acting as Assessors) found that the casualty was due to the gas from 405 tons of coal, which was stowed in the lower main-hold for the ship's use, having been allowed to accumulate in the 'tween decks, there being no ventilation whatever from either the main-hold or the 'tween decks, and to a light having been taken into the 'tween decks when the air was in a highly explosive state. The Court were also of opinion that ventilating shafts fitted with cowls, causing a continual current of air over the surface of the coal, would effectually prevent such explosions. Four lives were lost by the casualty.

1 796.   10,000.—11,78.   Wt. 10951.   E. & S.

FISHING VESSELS

'Ye are especially to consider of the whole business of fishing of these our kingdoms or any

113. Wick Harbour during herring fishing, 1875.

of our distant dominions or plantations ...' said the *Instructions for the Council of Trade* appointed on November 7th, 1660.

Fishing vessels were generally covered by the Merchant Shipping Acts, although with special provisions and exemptions. For example, they were exempt from load-line requirements, while specifications for the carriage of boats did not apply to vessels engaged in whaling. The British fishing fleet in the later 19th century consisted of relatively small craft working in an area not very different from home trade limits – apart from whalers in the Greenland waters.

More recently, the increase in size and range of trawlers, development of factory ships and relatively high loss of life, have resulted in changes to the legislation. Regulatory measures

have been extended to cover fishing vessels and also private pleasure craft. Fishing vessel survey offices examine and approve plans including stability of fishing vessels, structural fire protection and safety equipment, and crew accommodation. They also survey hull construction and machinery.

EMIGRATION

When William Huskisson was President of the Board he was in favour of workers having the freedom to emigrate and supported the 1825 measure that repealed restrictions. The Select Committee on Emigration from the United Kingdom recommended the grant of £50,000 to aid immediate emigration from the cotton-manufacturing districts to North America, for the transition of a power-loom weaving had proved disastrous for the hand-loom cotton weavers. A return printed in the *Parliamentary Papers* for 1830 states the total number of emigrants from the UK in the years 1821–29 to be: to the North American colonies 99,394; to the British West Indies 13,072; to the Cape of Good Hope 1,575; and to Australia 7,693.

Emigration was controlled by the Passenger Acts. It had been particularly high between 1846–54, which doubtless led to the passing of the first Passenger Act. The Board of Trade was concerned even then about the conditions of steamships carrying passengers, when it promoted the 1851 Steam Navigation Act. None of the Acts define an 'emigrant' and emigrants appear to have been regarded as synonymous with steerage passengers (ie any passengers other than cabin passengers). The administration of the Passenger Acts was transferred from the Emigration

114. Fishing vessels were generally covered by the Merchant Shipping Acts.

CAUTION.

FISHING VESSELS' LIGHTS.

DRIFT NET FISHING VESSELS.

To show how important it is for Fishing Vessels to carry the lights required by the regulations, the Board of Trade call attention to a recent case in which the master of a Steam Trawler was charged under the 4th Section of the Sea Fisheries Act, 1883, with failing to take all necessary steps to avoid damage to a fishing-boat through whose drift nets he had run, doing thereby considerable damage.

It was proved, however, that the Drift Net Fishing Vessel, although having her drift nets out, had, at the time of the accident, only *one white light* burning instead of the *two white lights* as required by Section 10 (b) of the regulations. No compensation could consequently be obtained, the master of the Steam Trawler naturally assuming that, as the Drift Net Vessel only showed *one white light*, she was not fishing with her drift nets.

The regulation is as follows:—

Article 10 (b). "All vessels, when engaged in fishing with drift nets, shall "exhibit two white lights from any part of the vessel where they can be best seen." "Such lights shall be placed so that the vertical distance between them shall be "not less than 6 feet, and not more than 10 feet; and so that the horizontal "distance between them, measured in a line with the keel of the vessel, shall be "not less than 5 feet, and not more than 10 feet. The lower of these two lights "shall be the more forward, and both of them shall be of such a character, as "contained in lanterns of such construction, as to show all round the horizon, on "a dark night with a clear atmosphere, for a distance of not less than three miles."

By order of the Board of Trade,

18th November, 1885.   THOMAS GRAY.

Handbill № 61

Commissioners to the Board of Trade in 1872.
Part III of the Merchant Shipping Act 1894 gave
the Board power to appoint Emigration Officers
to administer the arrangements for transport of
emigrants. 'Emigration was regarded as a good
thing' remarked one writer, John Frost: 'It
certainly helped to deal with unemployment at
home and to spread British influence abroad'. It
is not clear when 'steerage' came to an end, but
the provisions were finally repealed in the
Merchant Shipping Act 1970.

115.   Emigrants
to America,
1890.

116.   Departure
of an emigrant
ship, 1850.

Carriage of crude oil is recognised as a potential, sometimes actual, threat to marine safety and the environment. Under an international convention of 1954 it became an offence to discharge any persistent oil within 50 miles of any coast. The United Kingdom enforced this by the Oil in Navigable Waters Act in 1955, and extended the limits thereafter. Early in the 1960s growing concern about pollution from oil spillage at sea led to the Warren Spring Laboratory's responsibilities being widened to include marine pollution. The Laboratory has since dealt with a wide range of problems arising from oil spills at sea and on the shoreline. It evaluates mechanical methods of removal and chemical dispersants, and is also concerned with international regulations for the safe transport of bulk chemicals.

With the advent of very large crude carriers and combined carriers, the major pollution hazard was the concentrated outflow of possibly hundreds of thousands of tons of neat crude oil as the result of a casualty. The *Torrey Canyon* broke up in heavy seas on Seven Stones Reef, Cornwall in March 1967, with over 100,000 tons of crude oil on board. Oil fouled beaches all along the Cornish coast. In 1969 a UN agency, the Inter-governmental Maritime Consultative Organisation (now IMO – Inter-governmental Maritime Organisation) imposed even more stringent conditions on tankers and other ships.

Other potential sources of pollution are escapes from North Sea offshore oilfields and casualties concerning ships carrying dangerous goods in bulk. Current policy is to confine action to oil

117 & 118. *Torrey Canyon* stuck fast on Seven Stones Reef, off Land's End, 1967.

119. Dangerous chemicals being collected on Ventnor Beach, Isle of Wight, after an incident in 1980.

threatening pollution of coasts, coastal fisheries or to concentrations of sea birds. UK ships and aircraft must report any oil pollution accident or any ship seen discharging oil, and the position and nature of any slick. Reports are channelled to HM Coastguard and distributed by them to all interested parties. The operation of Marine division's plans to combat oil pollution were demonstrated when the *Amoco Cadiz* was wrecked on the Brittany coast in March 1978. Following the *Amoco Cadiz* accident, the Department of the Environment and the Department of Trade carried out a review of Britain's contingency arrangements and responses for dealing with oil spills. A Marine Pollution Control Unit under Rear-Admiral Stacey, was set up in Marine division and co-operates closely with the Coastguard Service. It is responsible for national contingency arrangements for controlling oil and chemical pollution, and advises local authorities on cleaning up pollution onshore.

OFFSHORE INDUSTRY: OIL AND GAS

All sorts of craft, never envisaged when the main Merchant Shipping Acts were drafted, now inhabit the North Sea. Some, such as rigs, cannot really be classed as ships, but can still create hazards for other ships and their own employees. The Inter-departmental Committee on Marine Safety was formed in July 1976 and chaired by the head of Marine division of the Department of Trade (since 1983, Transport) with members drawn from several other government departments. It co-ordinates regulations made under offshore, marine and industrial safety legislation, implementation of policy relating to safety at sea, develops policy on enforcement,

including inspection methods and inquiry procedures, and keeps international requirements in IMO and the International Labour Organisation under review.

THE COASTGUARD

The original Coastguard service was set up under the Board of Customs in 1822 with prevention of smuggling its primary purpose. At that time 50 per cent of all spirits drunk in the country were

120.
Coastguard
instruction.

estimated to be contraband. Lifesaving was a secondary consideration, and in those days the responsibility of the Board of Trade, although coastguards were expected to help ships in trouble and save the shipwrecked. In 1866 the service came under the control of the Admiralty, to make better provision for defence of the coasts, and the 'more ready manning of the Navy and protection of the revenue'. At that time the scale of pay for lifesaving by use of apparatus issued by the Board of Trade was two shillings, reduced to one shilling if life wasn't saved. The lack of adequate lifesaving equipment meant that often passengers and crew would drown just offshore in front of the helpless watchers, until George Manby invented his mortar which would fire a shot with 500 yards

121.   Rescue by breeches buoy from the shipwrecked French trawler *Jean Gougy,* 1962.

of line from shore to ship. Thereafter, the development of other types, including the Boxer rocket and Schermuly's pistol rocket apparatus improved lifesaving considerably.

By the mid–19th century smuggling was a less frequent occurrence, and the Coastguard had become a reserve force for the Navy. Responsibility for the service remained with the Admiralty until 1923 when it came directly under the Board of Trade. The 1922 Committee set up to investigate peace-time duties recommended that the Board of Trade should establish a 'coast watching force' to perform coastguard duties in connection with saving life, wreck salvage and administration of the foreshore. By 1930 coastguards' pay was 32 shillings a week and the cost to the country of running a professional lifesaving service was £180,000 a year. During World War II the Coastguard was first transferred to the Ministry of Shipping and then to the Admiralty and Ministry of War Transport. It returned to the Board of Trade in the mid-1960s.

A major reorganisation of the service was carried out in the 1970s, and Coastguard officers

122.   Manby's mortar.

123.
Coastguard
rescue gear.

124. Rescue
teams used
carts – hand or
horse-drawn,
to transport the
heavy life-
saving
apparatus in
the nineteenth
century.

125. Rescue
by Boxer
rocket, c.1880,
probably in the
Scilly Isles.

now direct operations from rescue centres equipped with the newest technology and communications. There are six maritime rescue co-ordination centres which, in 1984, controlled action in nearly 5,000 incidents ranging from major shipping disasters to rescues of people stranded on cliffs. The Coastguard service has its own helicopter and can call on others for help. The service was transferred to the Department of Transport in 1983, with all the other shipping and marine safety functions.

126. *The Cromdale* breaking up on the rocks at the Lizard, Cornwall, 1913.

The Board of Trade and Civil Aviation

WHEN the Ministry of Aviation was abolished, the Board of Trade was put in charge of civil aviation. Under its umbrella were accident investigations, air safety regulations, the nationalised air corporations, airports, and the formulation and direction of civil aviation policy. Last, but not least, came the National Air Traffic Control Service.

'The principal objective of civil aviation policy must be to encourage the provision of air services by British carriers, in satisfaction of all substantial categories of public demand, at the lowest levels of charges consistent with a high standard of safety, an economic return on investment and the stability and development of the industry...' *Civil aviation policy*. Cmnd 4213, 1969.

The Board of Trade represented Britain's interests with the International Civil Aviation Organisation, and dealt with negotiation of overseas air traffic rights. It had general oversight of British airline operators and licensed British airports. As well, it kept a watch on the safety performance of UK airlines. Its Directorate General of Safety and Operations was responsible for maintaining internationally agreed air safety standards, its work being complemented by that of the Air Registration Board, which held delegated responsibility to deal with air-worthiness matters. The Board issued operators' certificates and the staff of the Civil Aviation Flying Unit set standards of fitness, technical knowledge and flying experience for pilots and were also responsible for training and testing the standards of commercial flying instructors.

Responsibility for investigating aircraft accidents in the UK and accidents abroad to civil

127.   Exhibition at Festival Hall, 1969. Anthony Crosland (President 1967–69) is on the right.

128.   An HS748 turbo-prop aircraft in the Board of Trade fleet, 1970.

aircraft registered in the UK, belonged to the Accidents Investigation Branch. This was formed in 1919 as a result of public concern about the number of aircraft accidents then occurring. The Air Navigation Act 1920 required the Minister for civil aviation to make regulations providing for accident investigation, and in 1922 the branch became part of the Air Ministry. It was a part-military organisation, concerned mainly with military aircraft accidents, because civil air transport was then in its infancy. After World War II the branch transferred to the Ministry of Transport and Civil Aviation. It went to the Department of Transport from the Department of Trade and Industry in 1983, but as an Inspectorate it has always been quite independent of any policy-making division or regulatory

129. Air traffic control tower at Heathrow.

authority, and its Chief Inspector reports direct to the Secretary of State.

The 1967 Committee of Inquiry into Civil Air Transport (the Edwards Committee) was set up to investigate the economic and financial situation, and the prospects of the British civil aviation transport industry, also methods of regulating competition and licensing. It found the basic weakness to be a lack of clarity about policy objectives and lack of suitable machinery for action. The government set out its views on the necessary changes. These were to include the merger of BOAC and BEA, and the formation of a 'second force' airline by the private sector of industry – now British Caledonian. Much of the civil aviation work carried out by the Board of Trade was to be taken over by a new Civil Aviation Authority having responsibility for 'the whole spectrum of economic, operational and technical regulation ... for air-worthiness and for the non-military aspect of the air traffic control services'. The Authority was established as a body corporate, governed by a board appointed by the Board of Trade. However, international and general civil aviation policy, legislation in the safety, technical and operational fields, and noise abatement regulation remained with the Board of Trade.

CONCORDE

The Department of Trade and Industry took over the Concorde aircraft project in 1971, although the contracts were administered by the Ministry of Aviation Supply, and later by the Procurement Executive of the Ministry of Defence. An Anglo-French agreement had been signed in November 1962 to develop and produce jointly a civil

130. Trident
disaster 1972.

131. Concorde, 1985.

supersonic transport aircraft in medium and long-range versions. The two countries were to share the work, expenditure and proceeds of sales thereafter. Estimated costs were £150–£170 million in 1962, and rose massively as work proceeded. The aircraft went into service in 1976. Improved operating results showed a surplus of £10.2 million in 1982–83. Joint Anglo-French studies at that time confirmed the possibility that the British contribution to Concorde's support in-service could in future be met out of surpluses earned by Concorde's airline operations.

THIRD LONDON AIRPORT

The Commission on the Third London Airport, presided over by Mr Justice Roskill, broke new ground as a Committee of Inquiry. It was set up in May 1968 to investigate the timing of the need for a four-runway airport to cater for the growth of traffic at existing airports serving the London area, and to consider the various alternative sites. This marked a change from the white paper of the previous year which had concluded that development of Stansted Airport should be carried out. The Commission made extensive use of cost/benefit analysis as the 'best available aid to rational decision making'. At each stage of the Commission's work, the Board of Trade published material from public and local hearings, from written and oral evidence, and specially commissioned research studies.

The cost/benefit analysis was one of the most ambitious ever undertaken in the UK. Although the Committee's recommendations were ultimately rejected by the government, the text is still used by students of economics – and of English! Since the Roskill final report was published in 1971 other airport planning inquiries have been carried out. In Summer 1985, the government announced that Stansted was, after all, to be London's third airport and its capacity was to be increased initially to up to eight million passengers a year. It was announced at the same time that the British Airports Authority was to be privatised. By then, in 1983, civil aviation policy had been transferred to the Department of Transport.

Consumer Protection and Prices

THROUGHOUT its life the Board of Trade has had an interest in what affects the consumer, as well as the trader, having a hand in such matters as accuracy and standardisation of weights and measures, the price of food and other commodities, proper running of companies and fair trading.

In 1919 the rationing of some foods, imposed in 1918, was ended but profit controls remained and the Profiteering Act was passed. There were various attempts between the wars to legislate on consumer protection and prices, but little came of them. The Profiteering Act was repealed when the boom was over and prices tumbled, and a Food

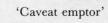
'Caveat emptor'

Council appointed by the Prime Minister in 1925 was not a statutory body. However, its investigations into short weight and measure on the sale of food made at the Board of Trade's request resulted in the Sale of Food (Weights and Measures) Act 1926.

A landmark in the history of British consumer protection came with the appointment of the Molony Committee in 1959. Although its remit did not include nationalised industries or services, its 1962 report made a series of recommendations on product safety, standards and comparative testing, labelling, redress in the civil courts for consumer complaints, trade descriptions and advertising. The establishment of the Consumer Council was part of the governmental response to the findings. The Council published an annual report and monthly magazine (*Focus*), and leaflets on various consumer topics until its generally unpopular abolition in 1970. In 1964 the Resale Prices Act abolished resale price maintenance, and during the 1970s there was a spate of consumer protection legislation on, for example, sale of goods, consumer contracts, credit and estate agents.

The Fair Trading Act 1973 established the Office of Fair Trading with a director general appointed by the Secretary of State. The same year saw the setting-up of the Price Commission under the Counter-Inflation Act, in a period of high and accelerating inflation, which laid down that price increases and profits should be monitored and controlled under a price code. In

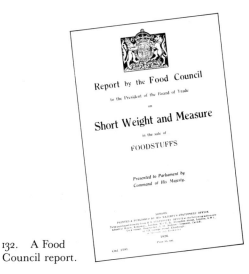

132. A Food Council report.

1975 the National Consumer Council was founded.

In March 1974 the Department of Prices and Consumer Protection, under a Secretary of State, took over responsibility for policy in these areas from the then defunct DTI, and food prices policy from the Ministry of Agriculture, Fisheries and Food. Its responsibilities included fair trading; standards, weights and measures; monopolies, mergers and restrictive practices; home and consumer safety; consumer credit; and competition policy.

Government policy since 1979 has been to promote a better deal for consumers through competition rather than regulation. In 1979 the new administration merged the Department of Prices and Consumer Protection with the Department of Trade, with a Minister for Consumer Affairs. The Competition Act 1980 abolished the Price Commission.

The Consumer Affairs division of the Department of Trade and Industry now has general responsibility for consumer protection matters, the nationalised industry consumer consultative councils and government support for the Citizens Advice Bureaux service. It liaises with the Office of Fair Trading on certain consumer legislation, and with the trading standards departments of local authorities, and sponsors the advertising industry. The Home Accident Surveillance System was set up in January 1977, with 20 hospitals co-operating in a scheme which aims to provide regular, comprehensive and nationally representative information on the causes of domestic accidents. The Department's Consumer Safety Unit now runs the system, and looks after safety concerning consumer goods, including fireworks.

The Consumer Credit Act 1974 was enacted as a result of the Crowther Committee's 1971 report on consumer credit. The Act brought within statutory control many types of credit business, including banking, mortgages, credit cards, debt collecting and credit reference agencies. All these must be licensed by the Office of Fair Trading.

133.   Consumer education material

134.   Winners of the Fireworks Safety Poster competition with Alex Fletcher, when Minister for corporate and consumer affairs, outside the House of Lords, 1983.

The Board of Trade in World War I

THE Great War spurred a sudden massive increase in state direction in a hitherto *laissez faire* economy. It had a marked impact on the administrative work of the Board, causing an almost complete break in the ordinary routine, and most of the staff not on active service were moved to war duties. Hubert Llewellyn Smith wrote that the labour exchanges and Unemployment Insurance department became a great recruiting agency for munitions workers, the Marine department took on war risks insurance and the maintenance of overseas communications, the Railway department was occupied with railways and coal mines and the Commercial department

'When a war of this magnitude breaks out, the President of the Board of Trade should immediately be made Joint Secretary of State for War, Supply Department' Kitchener to Walter Runciman. Quoted in: *A man of push and go: the life of George Macauley Booth,* by Duncan Crow. Hart-Davis, 1965.

with trading with the enemy and blockade questions. The Companies and Bankruptcy departments administered the emergency laws relating to enemy property, businesses and indebtedness and the Statistics department looked after food supplies.

At different stages in the war, emergency ministries took over more of the Board's work. These included the Ministries of Munitions, of Shipping and of Food. At the outbreak of war the Admiralty was given power to requisition ships. The Board of Trade dealt with insulated space on ships for foreign meat supplies and with, for example, the arrangements for supplying the

135. Women munition workers: 'They are not so strong as the men ... but what they lack in strength they make up in patriotic spirit'. Mrs Humphrey Ward: *England's effort.* 1916.

Mediterranean Expeditionary Force. The Board, liaising with the War Office, undertook the first large-scale operation involving the supply of refrigerated goods. Both the Admiralty and the Board shared the management of captured ships put to work for British trade. Shipbuilding was not, at that time, under any sort of control, which was perhaps surprising, considering the heavy losses from U-boat attacks.

By the end of 1916, the Board of Trade had relinquished many of its responsibilities, although only its labour functions were permanently lost. For the rest of the war its operations were mainly in the area of civil trade and industry. A number of temporary departments within the Board

administered war controls on coal, timber, paper, cotton, tobacco and petrol, and looked after canals and tramways. The Ministry of Labour, created in 1917, was given responsibility for labour exchanges and the Unemployment Insurance department.

The coalfields were also taken over in 1917 and production, prices and distribution, management and development of collieries, and employment of miners were organised by a Coal Controller through the Mines department within the Board of Trade.

A Committee was set up in December 1916 on the reorganisation of British commercial intelligence and whether foreign trade could be

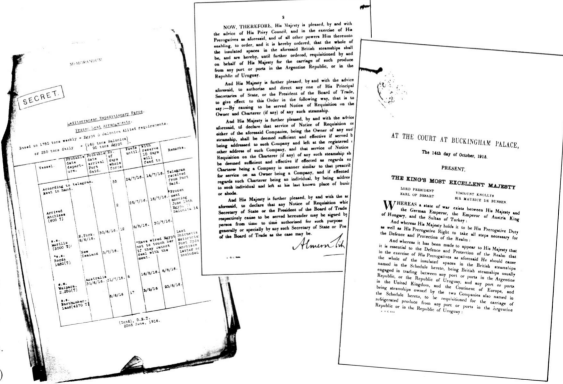

136. Secret plans for the first large scale operation of the war involving supply of refrigerated goods. (From B.T. 13-65/15 and 65/13.)

promoted by reform of the consular service. The Committee advocated the use of commercial intelligence counsellors 'to investigate conditions, analyse their causes, [and] observe recent changes'. At the end of 1917 the Department of Overseas Trade, jointly responsible to the Foreign Office and the Board of Trade, came into being, with delegated power to carry on the work of collecting and disseminating commercial intelligence, and to administer the overseas commercial services. A Petrol Control department was added to the Board in 1916, later to become the department responsible for controlling petrol distribution for civil and industrial purposes; this lasted until late in 1920.

137. The song played by Lloyd George is 'Keep the home fires burning', one of the most popular of World War I, 1917. The cartoon refers to the contemporary panic and hoarding of goods in short supply.

138. Board of Trade Roll of Honour, 1914–1919.

The Board of Trade between the Wars

EARLY in 1916 the President of the Board of Trade had appointed a number of departmental committees to consider the probable state of various important sectors of British industry after the war 'especially in relation to international competition' and to report what measures were necessary or desirable to safeguard that position. Industries examined included coal, iron and steel, engineering, electrical, shipping and shipbuilding, and the textile trades.

A memorandum from a departmental committee on the reorganisation of the Board of Trade in 1918 states: 'It is essential that steps should be taken forthwith to strengthen and improve the organisation of the Department with a view to affording the assistance required for the maintenance of our commercial and industrial position'. The creation of separate internal departments of Industries and Manufactures, of Statistics and of Public Services Administration in 1918 followed the recommendations of the reorganisation Committee, but a new department for Power and Transport was shortlived because the Ministry of Transport (1919–41) took over responsibility for railways and ports, canals, tramways and electricity supply.

The war had seen a great upsurge in support for state intervention and planning, and this had

> 'The great task of assisting in the restoration of our trade and industries after the war, which will largely fall upon the Board of Trade, depends for its success on the closest co-operation with the business community'. Sir Albert Stanley (later Lord Ashfield) in *Board of Trade Journal* 3 January 1918.

led to many institutional changes, such as new ministries, and increased government powers over the economy. The desire to get back to normal (ie a non-interventionist state) coupled with the alliance of Lloyd George with the Conservatives in the 1918 election meant that these experiments were soon abandoned. By 1921 most of the controls had been dismantled. So, despite the reports of the Ministry of Reconstruction (set up in 1917) little happened, in contrast to plans drawn up during World War II, which were followed through in peacetime.

The Board had several post-war tasks. It demobilised the energy ministries and departments within and outside the Board, and wound up war activities. It inherited the duties of the former Ministries of Food and of Shipping (which now included responsibility for military transport) and of the War Trade Department; it also dealt with the liquidation of war problems with contracts and industrial property. Sea transport and Coastguard services were passed to the Mercantile Marine department of the Board in 1923 and the new Mines department was attached to the Board, although internally autonomous.

In 1919 the government established the Export Credits Scheme under which it guaranteed bills drawn by exporters, and set up ECGD. The

139. Board of
Trade, Great
George Street,
1920-1940.

140. The mining industry strike in 1926 had a severe effect on the fishing fleet; many trawlers and liners were laid up because of the shortage of coal.

British Industries Fairs of 1920 and later were increased in scope. During the war, the 'knowledge that the country's first duty was to produce munitions led the Board of Trade to prohibit firms who were mainly engaged in the production of war requirements from exhibiting at trade fairs and practically confined the fairs to a few non-essential trades'. (*Board of Trade Journal supplement*, August 1919.)

Legislation enacted during the 1920s promoted a degree of protection and subsidy to British industry. The Committee on textile trades, appointed by the Board to consider the industry's position after the war, recommended that importation of foreign dyes should be prohibited except under licence. The war had revealed that four-fifths of dyestuffs were imported from Central Europe – and dyes like aniline were needed to

THE LABOUR CABINET. 1929

BACK ROW
RT. HON. GEORGE LANSBURY. COMMISSIONER OF WORKS.   RT. HON. A. V. ALEXANDER. ADMIRALTY   RT. HON. SIR C. P. TREVELYAN. BOARD OF EDUCATION.
RT. HON. MARGARET BONDFIELD. MINISTER OF LABOUR.   RT. HON. LORD THOMSON. SECRETARY FOR AIR.   RT. HON. TOM SHAW. SECRETARY FOR WAR.
RT. HON. ARTHUR GREENWOOD. MINISTER OF HEALTH.   RT. HON. NOEL BUXTON. MINISTER OF AGRICULTURE   RT. HON. WILLIAM GRAHAM. PRESIDENT OF BOARD OF TRADE
RT. HON. WILLIAM ADAMSON. SECRETARY FOR SCOTLAND.

FRONT ROW
RT. HON. J. R. CLYNES. HOME SECRETARY.   RT. HON. LORD PARMOOR. LORD PRESIDENT OF THE COUNCIL.   RT. HON. J. H. THOMAS. LORD PRIVY SEAL.
RT. HON. PHILLIP SNOWDEN. CHANCELLOR OF THE EXCHEQUER   RT. HON. J. RAMSAY MacDONALD. PRIME MINISTER   RT. HON. ARTHUR HENDERSON. FOREIGN SECRETARY
RT. HON. LORD PASSFIELD. DOMINION SECRETARY.   RT. HON. LORD SANKEY. LORD CHANCELLOR.   RT. HON. WEDGEWOOD BENN. SECRETARY FOR INDIA.

141.   William Graham with President of the Board of Trade 1929-31. Third from the right is Sidney Webb, President in 1924.

produce khaki uniforms! The Dyestuffs Import Regulation Act 1920 and the Safeguarding of Industries Act 1921 followed. Tariffs could be imposed to protect key industries and counteract the practice of dumping, and the Board resumed a limited responsibility for tariff matters. A Committee on industry and trade was set up in 1924 to report on conditions and prospects for British industry and commerce, with special reference to the export trade.

This period saw increasing industrial decline, unemployment and industrial disputes, culminating in the General Strike of May 1926,

and eventually in the great depression. The 1920s had a permanent pool of over one million unemployed. At the Ottawa Conference in 1932 a new system of tariffs and imperial protectionism was inaugurated to encourage manufacture and provide a bargaining counter in tariff negotiations. The idea was 'imperial free trade' between Britain and her colonies and the dominions, although more general free trade remained the ideal. The Import Duties Act of that year imposed a general tariff of 10 per cent on all imports other than those scheduled in a free list (which included most food and imports from the dominions). An independent Import Duties Advisory Committee, chaired by Sir George May (who had chaired the inquiry into public expenditure in 1931 which called for massive cuts and led to the downfall of the Labour government), carried out this work and could impose a tariff of up to a third in favour of any industry requesting it. The Board of Trade had the task of negotiating bilateral trade agreements with other countries.

Premonitions of impending war affected the Board of Trade as it did others in the 1930s. In 1936 a Food (defence plans) department was established in the Board 'to prepare in advance plans for execution by the Board of Trade immediately on the outbreak of war and by the Ministry of Food as soon as constituted'. The Food department, under Henry French, established liaison with the food trades, and its distribution branch planned a rationing scheme to hold wartime supply level with demand.

BOARD OF TRADE ADVISORY COUNCIL

This was a standing advisory body established to keep the Board informed of current trends and developments in industry, commerce and finance at home and overseas. Its members included the chairmen of the chief trade and industrial organisations and representatives of all the principal industries, branches of commerce, finance and labour, other government departments, and from the dominions. The Council met monthly, with the President in the chair, to review and discuss the current situation in the light of surveys supplied by Council members and the most recent official information.

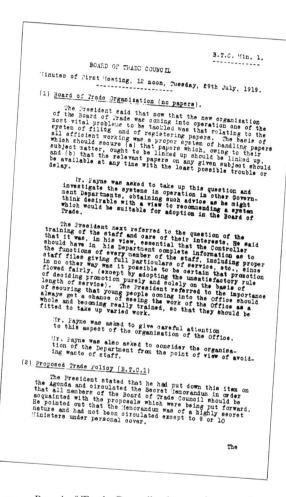

142. Board of Trade Council minutes, first meeting, 1919.

The Board of Trade in World War II

I N World War II the Board of Trade was responsible for trade at home, and administered the control of materials and production, certain forms of rationing, and enemy property. During the period after Munich and before the start of war, its sections dealing with food, fuel and petrol finalised their control plans. However, most of this war planning was going on in those sections of the Board that were to become new ministries

'There is enough and to spare for all if we have *fair shares*. Rationing is the way to get fair shares.' *Board of Trade advertisement,* 1941

when war actually began. In 1939 the Food department of the Board was made an independent ministry. A Ministry of Shipping was established, which took over the shipping work of the Board and, for a short while, merchant shipbuilding, although this responsibility was passed to the Admiralty in 1940.

The Mines department began to seek ways of restricting coal consumption and planned a

143. View of London, April 1939, before the bombing raids; the Board of Trade is in the centre.

scheme which included consumer rationing, divisional coal offices and local fuel overseers to watch over distribution. Board of Trade officials devised differential rationing schemes for various categories of user.

Unlike World War I, rationing and other powers were assumed at the start of hostilities. The day after enactment of the Emergency Powers (Defence) Act 1939, regulations were issued giving the Board powers to regulate or prohibit production, storage, distribution or consumption of any article or commodity, to license business transactions, control prices, and

introduce and operate control schemes. The Industrial Supplies department of the Board (set up in 1939) ensured that all available production capacity was devoted to the essential home and export trade.

A memo by the Department of Overseas Trade, written in August 1939, set out the aims of the export trade in wartime: to earn foreign exchange; to retain goodwill in overseas markets; to exploit opportunities provided by the elimination of enemy countries; and to maintain employment in non-war industries. In 1940 the President set up the Export Council, with the aim of promoting 'the greatest volume of export trade which can be achieved under the conditions of war ... the maintenance of export trade is so vital a factor in the war effort of the allied powers that no measure calculated to contribute to the end in view should be excluded from consideration'. There were to be export committees in individual industries; liaison would be arranged with the Board of Trade for supervising the day-to-day operations; and machinery created to deal with the allocation of raw materials for export orders

145. Clothes rationing was introduced in 1941.

144. Girl with bobbins at a cotton mill, 1939.

under plans worked out with the Ministry of Supply.

At the beginning of the war there were no immediate plans for clothes rationing. However, war orders and increased civilian buying led to a rise in textile and clothing prices; imports of cotton from the United States had increased, while export orders were being turned down by British textile manufacturers. The Industries and Manufactures department considered this unsatisfactory state of affairs, and early in 1940 proposed that sales of cotton material and clothes to retailers be cut by 25 per cent so that cotton piece-goods and made-up goods would again be available for export. This was approved and extended to other materials. The quota was fixed at 25 per cent of pre-war for linen and 75 per cent for cotton and rayon.

Soaring prices led to the anti-profiteering Prices of Goods Act 1939. This authorised the Board to appoint a Central Price Regulation Committee and local committees, and to designate price-regulated goods with prices kept at or rolled back to August 1939. However, it was 1 June 1941 before the immediate rationing of clothes, including footwear, was announced. Each person was to have 66 clothing coupons to last 12 months. 'We must learn, as civilians' said Oliver Lyttelton, when President of the Board (he later became Lord Chandos), 'that it is also honourable to be seen in clothes which are not so smart, because we are bearing, as civilians, yet another share in the war if we too are battle-stained' – a tradition that extended for many years after the war. In his autobiography, Lord Chandos reminisces: 'The most difficult part of the scheme on which to form a judgement was, of course, the total number of coupons which each person should have and, within this, the weighting to be given to each coupon. If one for a handkerchief, how many for

RATIONING of Clothing, Cloth and Footwear from June 1

There is enough and to spare for all if we have *fair shares*. Rationing is the way to get fair shares. *Fair shares*—when workers are producing bombs and aeroplanes and guns instead of frocks, suits and shoes. *Fair shares*—when ships must run the gauntlet with munitions and food rather than with wool and cotton. *Fair shares*—when movements of population outrun local supplies. Rationing is not the same as shortage. Rationing, or *fair shares*, is the way to *prevent* a shortage without interfering with full war production.

So, from now on (June 1st, 1941) you will have to present coupons to buy clothing, cloth, footwear and knitting wool. At present the coupons to be used are the Margarine Coupons in your Food Ration Book. (You don't need these for margarine, and it is a great saving of paper to use this page for the clothing ration.) There are 26 coupons on the margarine page. The numbers printed on them are to be ignored ; each coupon counts 1 only. You will receive 40 more coupons making 66 to last you *for a full year*.

How much will the coupons entitle you to buy ? Here are a few examples taken from the long list which will be printed in your paper to-morrow. *Watch out for this list !* A woollen dress will need 11 coupons, a man's trousers 8, a pair of socks 3, and 1 coupon will allow you to buy two han[...] collar, or two [...]

retailer will simply cut out the necessary number of coupons for you. *It is illegal to sell or buy coupons*—for this would defeat the purpose of " fair shares."

Special cases are being looked after. Hère are a few examples. Clothing for babies won't need coupons at all. Because children grow fast their clothes are rated at less coupons than grown peoples'. Mending wool, boiler suits, sanitary towels, elastic, hats, caps, and clogs are among the articles which you can buy without coupons. So are all second-hand articles. Blitzed households will be able to get special replacement coupons.

This rationing scheme is as much a surprise to your retailer as it is to you. Of course it had to be kept secret, or some people might have tried to get in first. It must take a few days to sort things out. You will lose nothing by postponing your purchase, because from to-day it is illegal, as well as [...] interest, for any [...]

CLOTHING AND FOOTWEAR RATIONED
66 COUPONS TO LAST FOR 12 MONTHS
CONCESSIONS FOR GROWING CHILDREN

The immediate rationing of clothing, including footwear, was announced yesterday by the Board of Trade. Each person will have 66 clothing coupons to last for twelve months, and these will have to be surrendered when clothes are bought.

Mr. Oliver Lyttelton, President of the Board of Trade, who announced the new scheme in a broadcast at 9 o'clock yesterday morning, emphasized that the plan is designed so that every one may have a fair share.

146. Board of Trade publicity for clothes rationing.

147. Wartime notices issued by the Board of Trade.

MAKE DO AND MEND LEAFLET. No. 14

CHILDREN'S UNDERWEAR BUYING AND REPAIR HINTS

"Keep them tidy underneath!"

says Mrs. SEW-and-SEW

It's quite a problem to keep children in underclothes. They give them such hard wear and grow out of them so quickly. Here are some practical hints which may help you keep them tidy underneath !

BUYING TIPS

★Never forget to allow for rapid growth. When buying ready-made underwear, always buy a size or more larger than needed.

When buying judge quality and workmanship by (a) well reinforced knicker forks and under-arms of vests. (b) good finish at edges of seams. These should be strong but soft to stand frequent washing and keep in shape, neither fraying nor chafing the skin. (c) Good button-hole finish and well-sewn seams.

ISSUED BY THE BOARD OF TRADE

PLEASE BRING YOUR OWN TOWEL

ISSUED BY THE BOARD OF TRADE

(21713D) W: 50790/6616 100m 3/43 H J R & L Gp 745/4

a pair of socks, or a shirt or a skirt?'

During the first two years that clothes rationing was in force, it is estimated that a quarter of a million tons of shipping space a year were saved, and 600,000 workers in the clothing industry released for the forces or for war work.

Early in 1942 the War Cabinet was faced with ordering further civilian economies – possibly cutting the clothes and petrol rations, as well as considering the rationing of household coal. The Board of Trade devised its utility cloth and clothing programme in 1941 to increase supply of cheap clothing that would meet the need for utility goods at low or moderate prices. Successive Orders set maximum prices and imposed various prohibitions for the clothing trades. In August 1942 purchase tax was removed from all utility clothing. Its production passed that of non-utility clothing early in 1942 and by 1943 it had risen to nearly 80 per cent of all civilian clothing production.

Under the government's austerity programme
the Board of Trade decided to reduce production
of civilian furniture below its 1941 level again, to
release more war workers. Furniture was already
scarce, many people needing replacements
because of bomb damage, and the problem was to
control production and distribution and to
improve quality at a lower price. The Board's
solution was to introduce standard designs and
specifications, set maximum prices, select firms to
make the utility furniture, allocate production
programmes and an appropriate quantity of raw
materials, and limit supply to priority groups.
Before the President announced the Utility
Furniture Scheme in July 1942 he had appointed a
Committee to design durable and attractive
furniture that would be reasonably priced,
soundly constructed and economical to produce.
Other rationing cuts were made by the Board on
household articles in short supply, and it licensed
a number of consumer industries with the

intention of restricting or standardising
production.

By the Autumn of 1942 fuel and power were
both within the Board's control. A Petroleum
department had been set up in May 1940 and
electricity powers returned from the Ministry of
War Transport in 1941, but the problem of
obtaining sufficient coal supplies led to proposals
to ration fuel and reorganise coal production, and
ultimately to the formation of a Ministry of Fuel
and Power in June 1942. Early that year the
President, Hugh Dalton, had announced that
rationing of domestic fuel would be introduced in
the Autumn, and Sir William Beveridge was
asked to work out a rationing scheme on the most
equitable and effective methods of restricting and
rationing fuel. This was subsequently published as
the white paper: *Fuel rationing*. It was vehemently
opposed in the House of Commons and was not
introduced.

Concentration of industry schemes promoted by

the Board from 1941 onwards enabled many thousands of workers to be released for war work from civilian industries between 1941–44. An expanded Industries and Manufactures department administered the Prices of Goods Act, Goods and Services (Price Control) Act 1941, Limitation of Supplies Orders, and the Location of Business Orders. From 1942 the Board had responsibility for policy and regulation of commerce and industry. It became an executive department, administering controls on prices, clothing and furniture. Speaking in Parliament, Dalton said: 'We have widespread powers of control over prices and price margins, particularly for consumer goods. Further, there has been growing up a habit of regular consultations between the Government and Trade and Industry, as a result of which there is a much better mutual understanding on both sides of the point of view of the other.'

The Board was also in charge, under the War Risks Insurance Act 1939 and the War Damage Act 1943 for war damage claims for chattels. This work was carried out by the Insurance and Companies department. In 1942 the Treasury and Board of Trade established the Trading with the Enemy department. It compiled registers of United Kingdom assets in enemy territory, assisted in the preparation of property clauses in the Peace Treaties and negotiated property agreements with allied governments.

The Board of Trade, by virtue of its close contact with producers and manufacturers during the war, subsequently became the vehicle for developing new attitudes in peacetime. As Dalton wrote, in a Board of Trade staff notice in September 1944: 'The Board of Trade has made an indispensable contribution to the war effort. We have been the chief instrument for restricting exports and civilian consumption and for ensuring, over a wide field, fair shares for our civilians in the restricted supplies. We have given … first priority to the claims of the Service and Supply Departments for labour, material, factory space and shipping. But we must now give a sharp jolt to all the mental habits of five years. We must cultivate, in all our dealings with civilian needs and exports, an expansionist, in place of a restrictionist, bias.'

149. Cargo loaded for New York at a British port, under the eyes of the Home Guard.

Post-War Years

I N 1951, when Sir Frank Lee became Permanent Secretary to the Board of Trade, he received a telegram from an old friend in the United States: 'Look after the Trade and the Plantations will look after themselves!' And that is just what happened. In the years after the war, the Board's main preoccupation was the need to expand exports, and it began to direct its course first towards export promotion, then to variants of the old British Industries Fair, with such attention-getting images as British Fashion Fortnight, and to export markets at large through the work of the British

> 'To be the Permanent Secretary of that Department is to have what I am confident is the most fascinating post in Whitehall' Sir Frank Lee.

National Exports Council.

Much-needed dollars came into the country with the assistance of the Dollar Exports Board. This was a non-governmental body supported with financial assistance from both government and non-official sources and set up by industry for industry. Industrialists who had achieved success in exporting to North America encouraged and helped others to do the same. 'The expansion of our exports to the USA – now our largest export market – is due in no small measure' said Sir Frank Lee in 1958, 'to the enthusiasm, the publicity, and the pooling of

150.   Harold Wilson and Sir Stafford Cripps at the Board of Trade canteen, 1945.

151.   Tobacco talks open at the Board of Trade between British and American negotiators, January 1949. Sir John Woods, Permanent Secretary, centre.

152. Trade mission leaving Northolt for China, 1946.

experience which the Council has brought to its task. It is one of the happiest creations of the Board in recent years.' The Advisory Council on Middle East Trade, also created by the Board of Trade, carried out a similar role.

The late 1940s and the 1950s saw many changes in the Board's work. It resumed its traditional role as the Department advising on industrial and commercial policy and external trade. With the rest of the Western trading world it set out to dismantle pre-war protectionism and commodity

cartels, replacing them with multilateral trade agreements such as GATT (General Agreement on Tariffs and Trade) which was signed in Geneva in 1947 by 23 countries. The GATT sought to do away with trade discrimination and protectionism. It was, said Sir Frank Lee, 'the basis for concerted and successful efforts to limit and bind tariffs over a wide area ... an imperfect instrument with which many people grow restive on many occasions – but can anyone doubt that there would be more impediments to world trade

153. Sir Frank Lee.

154. The uneasy balance between imports and exports in 1947 as seen by *Punch*.

if there were no General Agreement?'

Other liberalising rules for trade were brought in through the OEEC (Organisation for European Economic Co-operation) and EFTA (European Free Trade Area), and a series of international commodity agreements. Customs duties and quantitative restrictions were bargained away. The Import Duties Act 1958 repealed 'a whole jungle of pre-war tariff legislation' and provided a new tariff structure paving the way for use of the 'Brussels nomenclature'.

The Board was largely responsible for this legislation and the procedure of investigating, considering and making decisions on tariff

applications was vested in the Board rather than, as by the 1932 Act, in the Import Duties Advisory Committee – a body separate from any government department. Expressions like 'most favoured nation treatment' and 'non-discrimination' in simple terms meant that British negotiating teams, led by Board of Trade officials, were concluding pacts to open up world markets to competition and efficient supplies for the consumer.

In those years successive Presidents of the Board of Trade and their senior officials considered how the Board could contribute to the debates about balance of payments problems created by the competing demands of awakening prosperity at home and the need to earn our livelihood abroad. Currency crises and setbacks, such as the commodity supply crisis sparked off by the Korean War, demanded new policy initiatives or organisational improvisation, such as the shortlived Ministry of Materials. But essentially this was a time of growth and new ideas.

The old peacetime links were resumed by the Board's officials with Britain's closest trading partners; the Board's Trade Commissioners throughout the Commonwealth and the colonies were actively helping exporters and local investors. Officials from the Board's London headquarters were posted to major embassies, to the UK's permanent delegations to OEEC and GATT, and carried out negotiations in the UN Food and Agriculture Organisation or major commodity organisations. The EFTA convention was signed on 4 January 1960 by seven countries, the objectives being 'to promote in the area of the Association and in each member state a sustained expansion of economic activity, full employment, increased productivity and the rational use of resources, financial stability and continuous improvement in living standards; to secure that trade between member states takes place in conditions of fair competition...'

Meanwhile, on the home front, the Board was charged with five major lines of policy. First, revival of the economic fortunes of regions where the old heavy capital industries were dying – shipbuilding, mining, tinplate and later, the textile mills – by controls and incentives for locating new industrial development under the Distribution of Industry Acts; second, stimulating the old consumer industries under working parties and Development Councils for jute, lace, pottery, and furniture, and encouraging major restructuring with financial assistance for rationalising cotton textile capacity; third, fostering new ventures and promoting the industrial application of inventions and scientific developments through the National Research Development Corporation. Fourth, the Board sponsored industrial practices through the newly established British Standards Institution, the British Productivity Council, the British Institute of Management, and the Council of Industrial Design. Finally, it was responsible, as is its successor, for new legislation on companies, on monopolies and restrictive practices. The Monopolies Commission was established in 1948 and, in the early 1950s, a Royal Commission on Company Law was set up with a Board of Trade secretariat, preparatory to major new legislation.

These were years in which the Board resumed in no uncertain fashion its role in the economic debate at home, in international bargaining overseas, in the encouragement of domestic industry, and in regulation of the equitable conduct of business.

155.
Deputation to the Board of Trade on the problem of unemployment in South West Wales, meeting the President of the Board (Sir David Eccles), the Minister for Welsh Affairs (Mr Henry Brook) and the Minister of Power (Lord Mills) 1957.

The Board of Trade: 1960~70

By the terms of its original Order in Council, the Board of Trade had the task of overseeing all matters connected with trade and commerce. This remained true in the years after World War II. Based in Horse Guards Avenue until 1963–64, it continued to give high priority to overseas trade and exports. The Board maintained through the Commercial Relations and Exports divisions at home a network of commercial officers attached to British embassies abroad. It provided practical information for exporters, and administered tariffs

'The Board of Trade is not stuck up. There is no sense here, as there is in the Treasury, of clever men working in an ivory tower.' George Cyriax in *New Society,* October 1963.

and anti-dumping controls. To ordinary businessmen, officials at the Board were approachable; to them it was possibly the only approachable government department.

The Local Unemployment Acts 1960–66 enabled the Board to provide incentives to industrialists if they would locate or expand their businesses in the designated areas. They could purchase or rent factory premises from the Board (rent-free for a period), obtain building grants, and other aids such as higher investment grants, houses for key workers, training assistance and Regional

SSHargreaves   WATreganowan   WHartley   PJKSchwabe   RAWright   CaptALHawkins   HSChapman   SSimpson   HBWilliams   CFMarshall   WHSchwab.
Edward Leigh, F.I.B.P., F.R.P.S.   RVO   O.B.E   OBE RM   Cambridge.   O.B.E

HRWoodcraft   WPSOrmond   UHBetteridge   CWCubitt   The Rt Hon Edward Heath   WVSRobertson   RRCook   SHPerrin   WFCannon   DAWilson   ASWNewman
MBE SP   MBE   TD   MBE MP   CBE   SP   MBE SP   CBE
                              (V-Chairman)   (Chairman)   (V-Chairman)

156. Eastern Regional Board for Industry, 1st June 1964.

Employment Premium.

The 1960s saw many changes of responsibility in Whitehall: in 1964 the newly-formed Ministry of Technology took over several DSIR duties. Responsibility for shipping and shipbuilding was returned to the Board of Trade from the Ministry of Transport in the mid-1960s, but regional planning went in turn to the new Department of Economic Affairs, and telecommunications equipment to the Post Office. In 1966 the Board was given oversight of civil aviation matters.

An Introduction to the Board of Trade, issued in 1969, characterises its duties at that time as including: 'the maintenance of the right legislative framework to ensure a healthy environment in which commerce and industry can be efficiently and fairly operated; the maintenance of full and uniform employment throughout the country; the encouragement of exports towards a favourable balance of payments; the promotion of the well-being of the British shipping industry and marine safety [and] the British civil aviation industry and aviation safety; the provision of means of protection in the interests of the consumer ... for the inventor and designer [and] for the industrialist against foreign competition; a general survey of the economic environment; provision of a statistical service relating to the trade and industry of this country; the sponsorship of certain industries ...'

157. After the launch of the *Queen Elizabeth II* in 1967. She is being turned by the tugs to tow her to the fitting-out dock on the Clyde.

After the Board of Trade: 1970-79

I N 1970, when the Conservatives returned to power, a white paper was issued on the reorganisation of central government. The Board of Trade and Ministry of Technology were combined in one 'super-ministry' to be known as the Department of Trade and Industry, in order to unify commercial and industrial policy. The historic title of President of the Board of Trade was, however, retained by the new Secretary of State. The Ministry of Defence had absorbed the Admiralty, War Office, and Air Ministry in 1964, and in 1968, social policy was brought under the unified direction of DHSS. While the creation of the huge Departments of the Environment and of Trade and Industry was a continuation of this trend, it was also the result of a conscious philosophy of government organisation based on the 'functional principle' whereby similar functions are brought together under a single department (also to limit the size of the Cabinet). 'Government departments should be organised by reference to the task to be done or the objective to be attained'.

So the Department of Trade and Industry was responsible for most of the issues affecting industry and commerce – trade policy at home and overseas; marketing, investment and manufacture; design, research and development; service and manufacturing industries; public and private industry. Its main aim was to assist British

> '[Assisting] British industry and commerce to improve their economic and technological competitiveness'. *The reorganisation of central government.* Cmnd 4506, 1970.

industry and commerce to improve their technological strength and competitive-ness, and to look after government relations with the great majority of industries in both public and private sectors. In essence the DTI's aims

158. Lord Orr-Ewing visiting Metrication Board stand at the International Hardware exhibition, Olympia, February 1976.

were the same as they had been ever since the inception of the Board of Trade.

In 1971 policy responsibility for the aerospace industry, Rolls-Royce and Concorde went to DTI; in 1972 the British Overseas Trade Board was set up and in that same year a new ministerial position controlling industrial development was created. By this time DTI was in charge of trade and shipping, industrial development ranging from shipbuilding to small firms, the energy industries, overseas trade, commerce and consumer affairs and metrication. In January 1973 the United Kingdom, together with Denmark and Ireland, became a member of the European Community and Department officials began the regular round of trips to Brussels, Luxembourg and Strasbourg. In 1974 a new Department of Energy took over most of DTI's energy functions.

The changeover to a Labour government in 1974 meant changes also for DTI. It was split into three separate departments – Industry, Trade, and Prices and Consumer Protection, although they remained close together with shared support services. The Ministry of Posts and Telecommunications was dissolved, and its work given to the Department of Industry, and the National Enterprise Board was set up in 1976 with a large measure of operational and commercial freedom. This was Labour's agent of direct involvement in business without overt nationalisation of large parts of the economy.

By the end of 1974, the Department of Trade's preoccupations were, as were those of the old Board of Trade, commercial policy and commercial relations with overseas countries, and promotion of exports. The Department sponsored the UK shipping and civil aviation industries and regulated marine safety. It administered the basic legal framework for regulating industrial and

159. English language edition of the Official Journal

commercial enterprises, and the statutes governing company affairs and insolvency. It was also responsible for patents, trade marks, and copyright, and for the insurance industry. It sponsored tourism, the hotel and travel trade, newspapers, printing and publishing, the film industry, and other distributive and service trades.

EUROPEAN COMMUNITIES

Because of its longstanding involvement in the conduct of Britain's overseas commercial policy, our bilateral and multilateral obligations and our role as custodians of the large number of bilateral commercial agreements with other countries, the Board of Trade was particularly well placed to play a major role in the United Kingdom's approach to Europe.

The experience of Ministers and officials in the major rounds of multilateral tariff negotiations of the '40s and '50s, as well as the first attempt to establish a Europe-wide free trade area in the 1950s meant that the Board of Trade could contribute seasoned campaigners to the negotiating teams who went out to the first round of talks in the early 60s. It had been a Board of Trade Under secretary who had served as the UK's official observer at the negotiating conference under Paul-Henri Spaak which hammered out the ground rules of the Treaty of Rome.

In the 1960s round of negotiations the Board's ministers and officials made a major contribution to the discussions in Brussels and Whitehall, and to the exchanges with our Commonwealth partners about the progress made in those negotiations.

Although that attempt was frustrated by the first French veto, the lessons learned reinforced our understanding of the economic realities of Community membership, and the implications for the many aspects of Britain's industrial and commercial life for which the Board was answerable. The Board of Trade was perhaps uniquely qualified to evaluate the importance of the European market to the British manufacturer, against the background of the rapidly changing patterns of world trade. Over the period covered by the first and second French vetoes the Board maintained a steady flow of contacts, formal and informal, with the European Commission, the Council secretariat and the High Authority of the European Coal and Steel Community, about matters of common concern which were not confined to simple 'trade' or 'patent' questions, but went much wider. For example, in the aftermath of the ill-fated attempt to establish a European Technological Community in the late 1960s, the Board found itself closely involved in the discussions which led to the establishment of the organisation of multilateral technological research collaboration in Europe which, in turn, led to the Department acting as the Whitehall lead for coordinating the UK's contribution to establishing the European Community's policy for Research and Development.

Once the Government's intention had been clearly signalled to make a further attempt at joining the Community, it fell to the Department to furnish the greater part of the briefing on economic questions in the final negotiating conference, for Parliament and the public, as well as for the industrial and commercial community. It also had to provide negotiators not only for the main conference topics relating to the external commercial policy of the enlarged Community, but also for the wide range of secondary legislation to which we were to subscribe. This did not only cover such areas as insurance, export credits and competition policy, but also more abstruse subjects such as rights of establishment, and proof of good repute, which led into explorations of such matters as the legal powers of the Verderers of the Royal Forests, and the Swan Uppers of the Thames!

Nor did the work end with our accession to the Community. By common agreement, the negotiations for the UK's accession to the Generalised Preference Scheme in favour of developing countries was left till after our accession, and it fell to the Department to lead the negotiations that led to the establishment of the preference system of the enlarged Community, which became one of the most important elements

in the Community's policy for co-operating with
developing countries.

Over this period the Department also
established its own EEC Information Office which
provided information and guidance to exporters
and industrialists about the requirements of the
Community.

160.   Aerial view of the European Commission
building (Berlaymont — Centre) Brussels.

Beyond 1979

Although there were three separate departments up to 1979, they shared common services and staff moved from one department to another. In 1979 the Department of Prices and Consumer Protection was merged with the Department of Trade and the remaining two Departments were united in 1983 to form a new Department of Trade and Industry. At the same time responsibility for regulating use of radio frequencies was transferred from the Home Office, and aviation, shipping and marine matters were moved to the Department of Transport. Responsibility for small firms and tourism was transfered to the Department of Employment in 1985.

The re-creation of a single Department stresses the importance attached to the interests of commerce generally, and the new Department is responsible for services as well as manufacturing industries. Its central aim is to encourage, assist and ensure the proper regulation of British trade, industry and commerce, and to increase the growth of world trade and the national production of wealth . The restructuring of the Department is intended to further this objective by bringing together in one organisation those parts of government which deal most closely with industry. It makes little sense to erect artificial boundaries between manufacturing and service industries or between exports and home markets.

> 'To encourage, assist and ensure the proper regulation of British trade, industry and commerce ...' *DTI Aims.* 1984.

As Oliver Lyttelton said, long ago in 1945: 'There cannot be export policy in one compartment and trade policy for the home market in another'.

The DTI has three main areas of activity which are set out schematically in the DTI *Aims* booklet. First, it seeks to promote a climate for British industry which is as conducive to enterprise and competition as that in any other industrialised country. The DTI works closely with the

161. The aims of the DTI as developed by Norman Tebbit, Secretary of State for Trade and Industry, President of the Board of Trade, 1983–1985.

Treasury and other Departments to ensure that the needs of industry and commerce are taken fully into account when the priorities of government action are decided. It also represents the UK's industrial and commercial interests in the European Community, in other international organisations and in a wide range of bilateral relationships. This work helps companies to export successfully and underpins the Department's direct export promotion work.

The Department has been at great pains to establish the right regulatory framework to enable the market to function effectively, and this covers its traditional interest in company and competition law as well as patents and radio regulatory work. The DTI has responsibilities for the consumer, for safety legislation and for promoting and strengthening the British standards system. In exercising these functions it has to weigh the benefits of additional regulations against the burdens that may be placed on companies and particularly small firms. Finally in this area, the Department is responsible for regional policy and has a number of offices in the assisted areas to implement this as well as to ensure that its services are available to as wide a range of companies as possible.

The second area of the DTI's work is concerned with promoting the international competitiveness of British firms through increased efficiency and adaptability. The availability of skilled manpower is important for this, and the DTI works with other agencies to help improve training and to increase the industrial and commercial relevance of education at all levels. It has an interest in the improvement of management skills. Although specific responsibility for small firms now falls to the Department of Employment, many of DTI's activities are, of course, of considerable use to the

small firms sector and the DTI continues to take the needs of small firms into account in developing its policies. The Department continues its role in exports and co-ordinates all forms of government assistance for major projects overseas. The Export Credits Guarantee Department provides a wide range of credit insurance and related services for exporters.

The Department is also concerned with the structure of UK industry and government believes that the policy of privatisation will increase competitiveness. British Aerospace and Cable & Wireless have been returned to the private sector and the National Maritime Institute has been privatised. The flotation of British Telecom together with the liberalisation of the telecommunications market and the creation of OFTEL, are designed to stimulate new mass industries in communications and office systems. The Department also monitors the Post Office, British Leyland and British Steel and British Shipbuilders as well as Rolls Royce.

The final theme is innovation. The Department's support for innovation programmes offer companies assistance both for longer term research and development projects and for development work for new and improved products and processes. As well as having oversight of the Patent Office and sponsoring the British Technology Group, the Department has four major research establishments. These identify, develop and transfer to industry new technologies with widespread applications and have substantial duties in the metrology and standards area. The Department also co-ordinates the Alvey Programme, a major national research effort in advanced information technology. A key aim in the innovation area is the dissemination of best practice throughout industry, and the awareness and rapid adoption of key technologies has been promoted, particularly in new areas such as micro-electronics, information technology, biotechnology and advanced manufacturing as well as in quality control and design. The Department encourages closer co-operation between UK producers and their customers as one way of ensuring that new products meet the needs of the market.

The re-unification of the Departments of Trade and Industry is a change of some significance reflecting, perhaps, the objectives of the historic Board of Trade to encourage British commerce at home and abroad. So the wheel has come full circle from the 1786 Order that established the Board of Trade 'for the consideration of all matters relating to trade'.

162. Norman Tebbit, Secretary of State for Trade & Industry and President of the Board of Trade 1983–85, at the introduction of the Road-runner light truck, 25 September 1984.

163. Whitehall,
outside the
Board of
Trade, looking
north, 1842, by
T. Shotter
Boys.

Appendix A

Members of the Committee of Privy Council for the Consideration of all Matters Relating to Trade, 23rd August 1786.

The Lord Archbishop of Canterbury,
The First Lord Commissioner of the Treasury,
The First Lord Commissioner of the Admiralty,
His Majesty's Principal Secretaries of State,
The Chancellor and under Treasurer of the Exchequer,
  and The Speaker of the House of Commons,

should be members of the said Committee.
And that such of the Lords of His Majesty's Most

Honourable Privy Council as shall hold any of the following offices viz.:

The Chancellor of the Duchy of Lancaster,
The Paymaster or Paymasters General of His Majesty's Forces,
The Treasurer of His Majesty's Navy,
The Master of His Majesty's Mint,

should be members of the said Committee.
And His Majesty was at the same time pleased to order that the Speaker of the House of Commons of Ireland, and such persons as shall hold offices in His Majesty's

Kingdom of Ireland and shall be members of His Majesty's Most Honourable Privy Council in this Kingdom, should also be members of the said Committee. And His Majesty was further pleased to order that —

Lord Frederick Campbell,
Robert, Lord Bishop of London,
Lord Grantley,
Sir Lloyd Kenyon, Master of the Rolls (afterwards Lord Kenyon),
The Honourable Thomas Harley,
The Honourable Sir Joseph Yorke, KB (afterwards Lord Dover),
Sir John Goodriche, Bart.,
William Eden, Esq. (afterwards Lord Auckland),
James Grenville, Esq., and
Thomas Orde, Esq.,

should also be members of the said Committee. And His Majesty is hereby further pleased to Order that the Right Honourable Lord Hawkesbury, Chancellor of the Duchy of Lancaster, and in his absence, the Right Honourable William Wyndham Grenville, be President of the said Committee.

PRESIDENTS OF THE BOARD OF TRADE

BOARD OF TRADE (1786–1970)

1786	August	Lord Hawkesbury (became Earl of Liverpool in 1796)
1804	June	3rd Duke of Montrose
1806	February	1st Lord Auckland
1807	March	3rd Earl Bathurst *(below)*

164.

1809		Viscount Melville
1812		3rd Earl Bathurst
1815	September	2nd Earl of Clancarty
1818	January	Frederic Robinson (later Earl of Ripon)
1823	January	William Huskisson
1827	September	Charles Grant (later Lord Glenelg)
1828	June	W Vesey Fitzgerald
1830	February	J C Herries
1830	November	2nd Lord Auckland
1834	June	Charles Poulett Thomson (later Lord Sydenham)
1834	December	A Baring (later Lord Ashburton)
1835	April	Charles Poulett Thomson (later Lord Sydenham)
1839	August	Henry Labouchere (later Lord Taunton)
1841	September	Earl of Ripon
1843	May	William Gladstone
1845	February	Earl of Dalhousie
1846	July	Earl of Clarendon
1847	July	Henry Labouchere (later Lord Taunton)
1852	February	Joseph Henley
1852	December	Edward Cardwell (later Viscount Cardwell) *(below)*

165.

1855	March	Lord Stanley of Alderley
1858	April	Joseph Henley

| 1859 | March | 4th Earl of Donoughmore |
| 1859 | July | Thomas Milner Gibson (below) |

166.

1866	July	Sir Stafford Northcote, Bart (later Earl of Iddesleigh)
1867	March	6th Duke of Richmond
1868	December	John Bright *(below)*

167.

1870	January	Chichester Fortescue (later Lord Carlingford)
1874	March	Sir Charles Adderley (later Lord Norton)
1878	April	Viscount Sandon (later Earl of Harrowby)
1880	April	Joseph Chamberlain
1885	June	3rd Duke of Richmond and Gordon

| 1885 | August | Edward Stanhope *(below)* |

168.

1886	February	Anthony Mundella
1886	August	Sir Frederick Stanley (later Earl of Derby)
1888	February	Sir Michael Hicks-Beach (later Earl St Aldwyn)
1892	August	Anthony Mundella
1894	May	James Bryce (later Viscount Bryce of Dechmont)
1895	June	Charles Ritchie (later Lord Ritchie of Dundee)
1900	November	Gerald Balfour (later Earl Balfour)
1905	March	4th Marquess of Salisbury
1905	December	David Lloyd George (later Earl Lloyd George)
1908	April	Winston Churchill (later Sir Winston Churchill)
1910	February	Sydney Buxton (later Earl Buxton)

169. Sidney Buxton, President of the Board of Trade 1910-14, at his desk.

1914	February	John Burns *(below)*

170.

1914	August	Walter Runciman (later Viscount Runciman)
1916	December	Sir Albert Stanley (later Baron Ashfield)
1919	May	Sir Auckland Geddes *(below)*

171.

1920	March	Sir Robert Horne (later Viscount Horne)
1921	April	Stanley Baldwin (later Earl Baldwin)
1922	October	Sir Philip Lloyd-Greame (later Sir P Cunliffe-Lister, later Viscount Swinton, later Earl Swinton)

1924	January	Sidney Webb (later Baron Passfield)
1924	November	Sir Philip Lloyd-Greame (later Sir P Cunliffe-Lister, later Viscount Swinton, later Earl Swinton)
1929	June	William Graham
1931	August	Sir Philip Cunliffe-Lister, (formerly Sir P Lloyd-Greame, later Viscount Swinton, later Earl Swinton)
1931	November	Walter Runciman (later Viscount Runciman)
1937	May	Oliver Stanley
1940	January	Sir Andrew Duncan
1940	October	Oliver Lyttelton (later Viscount Chandos) *(below)*

172.

1941	June	Sir Andrew Duncan
1942	February	Col J J Llewellin (later Baron Llewellin)
1942	February	Hugh Dalton (later Baron Dalton)
1945	May	Oliver Lyttelton (later Viscount Chandos)
1945	July	Sir Stafford Cripps
1947	September	Harold Wilson (later Sir Harold Wilson later Lord Wilson of Rievaulx)

1951	April	Sir Hartley Shawcross (later Baron Shawcross)
1951	October	Peter Thorneycroft (later Baron Thorneycroft)
1957	January	Sir David Eccles (later Viscount Eccles)
1959	October	Reginald Maudling
1961	October	Frederick Erroll (later Baron - Erroll)
1963	October	Edward Heath (Secretary of State for Industry, Trade, Regional Development and President of the Board of Trade)
1964	October	Douglas Jay
1967	August	Anthony Crosland
1969	October	Roy Mason
1970	June	Michael Noble

DEPARTMENT OF TRADE AND INDUSTRY (1970-74)

The Department came into being on 20 October 1970 merging two previous departments: the Board of Trade and Ministry of Technology.

Secretary of State for Trade and Industry and President of the Board of Trade

1970	October	John Davies
1972	November	Peter Walker

DEPARTMENT OF TRADE (1974-83)

The Department of Trade and Industry was split into three new departments following the general election of February 1974.

Secretary of State for Trade and President of the Board of Trade

1974	March	Peter Shore
1976	April	Edmund Dell
1978	November	John Smith
1979	May	John Nott
1981	January	John Biffen
1982	April	Lord Cockfield

DEPARTMENT OF TRADE AND INDUSTRY (1983-)

Following the general election, the Prime Minister announced, on 11 June 1983, that the Departments of Industry and Trade would be merged to form the Department of Trade and Industry.

Secretary of State for Trade and Industry and President of the Board of Trade

1983	June	Cecil Parkinson
1983	October	Norman Tebbit
1985	September	Leon Brittan

Parliamentary Secretaries to the Board of Trade

The office of Parliamentary Secretary has existed during the whole of the lifetime of the Board of Trade (ie since 1786). Until 1867, the office holder was known as the Vice-President and thereafter as the Parliamentary Secretary. With the creation of the Department of Trade and Industry, following the general election of October 1970, the post was changed to that of the Parliamentary Under Secretary of State.

BOARD OF TRADE (1786-1970)

1786	August	W W Grenville
1801	November	Lord Glenbervie
1804	February	Nathaniel Bond
1804	June	George Rose
1806	February	Richard Chandos, Earl Temple
1807	March	George Rose
1812	September	Frederic Robinson
1818	January	Thomas Wallace (later Lord Wallace)
1823	January	Charles Grant (later Lord Glenelg)
1827	September	John Horton
1828	June	Thomas Lewis (later Sir T F Lewis, Bart)

1830	February	Thomas Peregrine Courtenay
1830	November	Charles Poulett Thomson (later Lord Sydenham)
1834	December	Viscount Lowther
1835	April	Henry Labouchere (later Lord Taunton)
1839	August	Richard Sheil
1841	June	Fox Maule (later Lord Panmure)
1841	September	W E Gladstone
1843	May	Earl of Dalhousie
1845	February	Sir George Clerk, Bart
1846	July	Thomas Milner Gibson
1848	May	Earl Granville
1852	February	Lord Stanley of Alderley
1852	February	Lord Colchester
1852	December	Lord Stanley of Alderley
1855	March	E Pleydell Bouverie
1855	July	Robert Lowe (later Viscount Sherbrooke)
1858	April	Earl of Donoughmore
1859	March	Lord Algernon Percy
1859	June	James Wilson
1859	August	William Cowper (later Lord Mount Temple)
1860	February	William Hutt
1865	November	G Goschen (later Viscount Goschen)
1866	February	William Monsell (later Lord Emly)
1866	July	Stephen Cave (later Sir Stephen Cave)

By the Act 30 and 31 Vict C 72 of 1867, the office of Vice-President was abolished and a Secretary with a seat in Parliament substituted.

1868	December	George Shaw-Lefevre (later Lord Eversley)
1871	January	A Wellesley Peel (later Viscount Peel)
1874	March	George Cavendish Bentinck
1875	November	Hon (later the Rt Hon) Edward Stanhope
1878	April	John Gilbert Talbot

1880	April	Hon Evelyn Ashley
1882	May	John Holms
1885	June	Baron Henry de Worms (later Lord Pirbright)
1886	February	C T D Acland (later Sir C T D Acland, Bart)
1886	August	Baron Henry de Worms (later Lord Pirbright)
1888	February	Earl of Onslow
1889	January	Lord Balfour of Burleigh
1892	August	Thomas Burt
1895	June	Earl of Dudley
1902	August	Andrew Bonar Law
1905	December	Hudson Kearley (later Viscount Devonport)
1909	January	H J Tennant
1911	October	J M Robertson
1915	May	E G Pretyman
1916	December	G H Roberts
1917	August	G J Wardle
1919	January	W C Bridgeman
1920	August	Sir P Lloyd-Greame (later Sir P Cunliffe-Lister)
1921	April	Sir W Mitchell-Thomson
1922	November	Viscount Wolmer
1924	January	A V Alexander
1924	November	Sir R Burton Chadwick
1928	January	Herbert Williams
1929	November	Walter Smith
1931	September	Gwilym Lloyd George
1931	November	Leslie Hore-Belisha
1932	July	Edward Burgin
1937	May	David Wallace
1938	April	Ronald Cross
1939	August	Gwilym Lloyd George
1941	January	Charles Waterhouse
1945	July	Ellis Smith
1946	January	J W Belcher
1949	January	L J Edwards
1950	March	Hervey Rhodes (later Lord Rhodes, see below)
1951	November	Henry Strauss
1955	April	Donald Kaberry

1955	October	Sir Derek Walker-Smith
1956	November	Frederick Erroll (later Baron Erroll)
1958	October	John Rogers
1960	November	Niall Macpherson (later Lord Drumalbyn)
1962	July	David Price
1964	October	Lord Rhodes
1967	January	Lord Walston
1967	September	Mrs Gwyneth Dunwoody

| 1974 | January | Cranley Onslow (appointed Parliamentary Under-Secretary for Aerospace Shipping and *Consumer Affairs*) |
| 1974 | January | Parliamentary Under-Secretaries of State reduced to *three* with move of Peter Emery (Industry) to Department of Energy. |

DEPARTMENT OF TRADE AND INDUSTRY (1970–74)

Parliamentary Under-Secretaries of State to the Department of Trade and Industry

1970	October	Appointment of *two* Parliamentary Under-Secretaries Antony Grant (Trade) Nicholas Ridley (Industry)
1971	April	Appointment of *third* Parliamentary under-secretary David Price (Aerospace)
1972	April	Lord Limerick (Patrick Edmund Pery, 6th Earl of Limerick) (Trade) (succeeded Antony Grant)
1972	April	Peter Emery (Industry) (succeeded N Ridley)
1972	April	Cranley Onslow (Aerospace) (succeeded D Price)
1972	April	Appointment of *fourth* Parliamentary Under-Secretary Antony Grant (Industrial Development)
1972	November	Cranley Onslow (appointed Parliamentary Under-Secretary for Aerospace and *Shipping*)

DEPARTMENT OF TRADE (1974–83)

Parliamentary Under Secretaries of State (PUSS)

1974	March	Eric Deakins	(Trade)
		Stanley Clinton Davis	(Companies, Aviation Shipping)
1976	April	Michael Meacher	(Trade)
1979	May	Norman Tebbit	(Civil Aviation, Marine, Shipping, Newspapers, Films, Publishing, Tourism, Hotels and Travel)
		Reginald Eyre	(Companies, Insurance, Insolvency, Patents Office, Distributive and Service Trades)
1981	January	Lord Trefgarne	(Succeeded N Tebbit)
1981	September	Iain Sproat	(Succeeded Lord Trefgarne)
1982	March	2nd Post as PUSS abolished	

DEPARTMENT OF TRADE AND INDUSTRY (1983–)

Parliamentary Under Secretaries of State (PUSS)

1983	June	Alex Fletcher	(Corporate and Consumer Affairs until September 1985)
1985	September	Michael Howard	(Corporate and Consumer Affairs)
		John Butcher	(Industry)
		David Trippier	(Industry) (From April 1985 Minister for Waste. From September 1985 transferred to Department of Employment).
		Lucas, Lord of Chilworth	(From September 1984 Department's spokesman in the Lords; Trade and Industry)

Secretary to the Department of Overseas Trade

This office was established under the Overseas Trade Department (Secretary) Act, 1918. The Act provided for the appointment of a Secretary of the Department of Overseas Trade (Development and Intelligence) 'who shall discharge the functions both of a parliamentary secretary to the Board and a parliamentary under-secretary to the Secretary of State.'

BOARD OF TRADE (1918–1970)

1918	February	Sir A Steel-Maitland
1919	July	Sir Hamar Greenwood
1920	April	F G Kellaway

1921	April	Sir Philip Lloyd-Greame (later Sir P Cunliffe-Lister)
1922	November	Sir William Joynson-Hicks
1923	March	Lt Col A Buckley
1924	January	W Lunn
1924	November	A M Samuel
1927	November	Douglas Hacking
1929	November	George M Gillett
1931	September	Edward Hilton Young
1931	November	David John Colville
1935	November	David Euan Wallace
1937	May	Robert Spear Hudson
1940	April	G H Shakespeare
1940	May	Harcourt Johnstone
1945	March	G S Summers

Secretary for Overseas Trade

1945	July	Hilary Marquand
1947	February	Harold Wilson
1947	October	A G Bottomley
1951	November	H Hopkinson
1952	June	H R Mackeson

Minister of State, Board of Trade

1953	September	Derek Heathcote Amory
1954	July	A R W Low
1957	January	Sir Derek Walker-Smith
1957	September	John Vaughan-Morgan
1959	October	Frederick Erroll (later Baron Erroll)
September 1962 appointment of *second* Minister of State		Lord Derwent
1963	October	Lord Drumalbyn (succeeded Lord Derwent)
1963	October	Edward du Cann (succeeded Alan Green)
1964	October	George Darling (succeeded Lord Drumalbyn)
1964	October	Edward Redhead (succeeded Edward du Cann)
1964	October	appointment of *third* Minister of State: Roy Mason

1965	October	Wilfred Brown, Baron Brown (succeeded E Redhead)
1967	January	Joseph Mallalieu (succeeded Roy Mason)
1968	April	Edmund Dell (succeeded G Darling)
1968	July	William Rodgers (succeeded J Mallalieu)
1969	October	reduction to *two* Ministers of State: Goronwy Roberts (succeeded Edmund Dell and William Rodgers)
1970	June	Frederick Corfield (sole Minister of State in Mr Heath's administration; succeeded Lord Brown and G Roberts)

DEPARTMENT OF TRADE AND INDUSTRY (1970–74)

Ministers of State

1970	October	appointment of *three Ministers of State* Lord Drumalbyn (Minister without Portfolio) Michael Noble (Trade) Sir John Eden (Industry)
1971	April	appointment of *fourth* Minister of State Sir Frederick Corfield (Aerospace)
1972	April	Thomas Boardman (Industry) (succeeded Sir J Eden)
1972	April	Michael Heseltine (Aerospace) (succeeded Sir F Corfield)
1972	April	appointment of *fifth* Minister of State Christopher Chataway (Industrial Development)
1972	November	Sir Geoffrey Howe (Trade and Consumer Affairs) (succeeded M Noble)
1972	November	Michael Heseltine assumed responsibility for Aerospace *and Shipping*

| 1974 | January | Ministers of State reduced to four with transfer of energy functions to Department of Energy |
| 1974 | January | Lord Aberdare (Minister without Portfolio) (succeeded Lord Drumalbyn) |

DEPARTMENT OF TRADE (1974–83)

The post of Minister of Trade was created following the general election of May 1979.

Minister for Trade

Special responsibilities for overseas trade, commercial relations and tariffs, Export Credits Guarantee Department, British Overseas Trade Board.

| 1979 | May | Cecil Parkinson |
| 1981 | September | Peter Rees |

The Department of Prices and Consumer Protection was merged with the Department of Trade following the general election of May 1979. The post of Minister for Consumer Affairs was created within the Department of Trade.

Minister for Consumer Affairs

| 1979 | May | Mrs Sally Oppenheim (Resigned February 1982) |
| 1982 | March | Dr Gerard Vaughan |

DEPARTMENT OF TRADE AND INDUSTRY (1983–)

Minister for Trade

| 1983 | June | Paul Channon |

Minister of State

1983	June	Kenneth Baker (Industry and Information Technology) September 1984 joined Dept Environment Norman Lamont (Industry)
1984	September	Norman Lamont (Industry September 1985, joined Ministry of Defence)
1985	September	Peter Morrison (Industry) Geoffrey Pattie (Information Technology)

Chief Permanent Secretarial Officers of the Board of Trade 1786–1927

1786 Aug. – 1825 May George Chalmers*
(Chief Clerk) *(below)*

173.

1825 July – 1836 Feb., Thomas Lack (Assistant
Secretary; after July 5,
1829, Joint Assistant Sec.)
1829 July – 1840 Jan., James Deacon Hume
(Joint Assistant Sec.)
1836 Feb., – 1841 June Sir Denis Le Marchant,
Bart. (Joint Assistant Sec.)
1848 May – 1850 Oct. Sir Denis Le Marchant,
Bart. (Joint Secretary)
1840 Jan., – 1847 Aug. John MacGregor (Joint Sec.)
1841 June – 1848 May Sir John Shaw Lefevre,
KCB (Joint Sec.)
1847 Aug. – 1852 Sept. George Porter (Joint Sec.)
1850 Oct. – 1865 Sept. James Booth (Joint Sec.)
1852 Sept. – 1866 Dec. Sir James Emerson
Tennent, Bart. (Joint Sec.)
1865 Oct. – 1866 Dec. Thomas Farrer
(afterwards Lord Farrer)
(Joint Sec.) *(below)*

1867 Jan. – 1886 May Thomas Farrer
(afterwards Lord Farrer)
(Sole or Permanent Sec.)
1886 May – 1893 May Sir Henry Calcraft, KCB
(Sole or Permanent Sec.)
1893 May – 1901 May Sir Courtenay Boyle, KCB
(Sole or Permanent Sec.)
1901 May – 1907 Jan. Sir Francis J.S.
Hopwood, GCMG,
KCB (afterwards Lord
Southborough) (Sole or
Permanent Sec.)
1907 Jan. – 1919 Aug. Sir H Llewellyn Smith, GCB
(Sole or Permanent Sec.)
1913 May – 1916 Mar. Sir G.S. Barnes, KCB,
KCSI (Second Secretary)
1916 Mar. – 1918 Jan. Sir W.F. Marwood,
KCB (Second Secretary)
1918 Jan. – 1919 Sept. Sir W.F. Marwood,
(Joint Secretary.)
1919 Aug. – 1920 Feb. Sir S.J. Chapman,
KCB, CBE (Joint Sec.)
1919 Sept. – 1920 Feb. Sir H.A. Payne, KBE,
CB (Joint Sec.)
1920 Mar. – 1927 July Sir S.J. Chapman,
KCB, CBE (Permanent Sec.)
1920 Mar. Sir H.A. Payne, KBE,
CB (Second Secretary)
1927 Aug. Sir Horace P. Hamilton KCB
(Permanent Sec.) *(below)*

174.

175.

NOTE: From 1786 to 1808 two Clerks of the Privy Council attended the Committee or Board as Secretaries, for which service they each received an additional £500 a year; although such payment ceased after 1808 the names of certain Clerks of the Privy Council appear in the Calendars as Secretaries until 1845.

176. Room on 2nd floor of Pembroke House, for several years occupied by the Permanent Secretaries to the Board of Trade 'Farrar's Room'.

BOARD OF TRADE (1927-70)

Permanent Secretary

1927	August	Sir Horace P Hamilton
1939	May	Sir William Brown
1941	February	Sir Arnold Overton
1945	August	Sir John Woods
1951	August	Sir Frank Lee
1959	November	Sir Richard Powell
1968	March	Sir Antony Part

2nd Permanent Secretary

1966	June	David Serpell
1968	December	Maxwell Palmer Brown

DEPARTMENT OF TRADE AND INDUSTRY (1970-74)

Permanent Secretary

1970	October	Sir Antony Part

2nd Permanent Secretary

1970	October	Sir Maxwell Palmer Brown (Trade)
		Sir Robert Marshall (Industry)
1972	April	3rd Second Permanent Secretary appointed Jack Rampton (Industrial Development)
1972	April	4th Second Permanent Secretary appointed Lawrence Tindale (Industrial Development)
1972	August	5th Second Permanent Secretary appointed Peter Thornton (Aerospace)
1972	November	Peter Thornton (Aerospace *and Shipping*)
1973	November	Peter Carey (succeeded Sir J Rampton)
		Sir Jack Rampton (succeeded Sir R Marshall)
1974	January	Reduction to 4 Second Permanent Secretaries. Sir Jack Rampton transferred to Department of Energy.

DEPARTMENT OF TRADE (1974-83)

Permanent Secretary

1974	March	Sir Maxwell Palmer Brown
1974	July	Sir Peter Thornton
1977	June	Sir Leo Pliatzky
1979	May	Sir Kenneth Clucas
		(Sir Leo Pliatzky remained on special duty prior to retirement)
1982	January	Michael Franklin (later Sir Michael Franklin)
1983	April	Sir Anthony Rawlinson

2nd Permanent Secretary

| 1974 | March | Sir Peter Thornton |
| 1974 | July | Post of Second Permanent Secretary abolished |

DEPARTMENT OF INDUSTRY (1974–83)

Permanent Secretary

1974	March	Sir Antony Part
1976	July	Sir Peter Carey
1983	May	Sir Brian Hayes

2nd Permanent Secretary

1974	March	Sir Peter Carey (Industry)
		Lawrence Tindale (Director of Industrial Development)
1974	July	Graeme Odgers (succeeding L Tindale)
1976	July	Anthony Rawlinson (succeeding P Carey)

| 1977 | July | A Rawlinson moves to Treasury. G Odgers retires |

Post of Second Permanent Secretary abolished.

DEPARTMENT OF PRICES AND CONSUMER PROTECTION (1974–79)

Permanent Secretaries

| 1974 | March | Kenneth Clucas |

DEPARTMENT OF TRADE AND INDUSTRY (1983–)

1983	June	Joint Permanent Secretaries appointed
		Sir Brian Hayes
		Sir Anthony Rawlinson (Retired March 1985)
1985	March	Sir Brian Hayes

177. Offices of the Board of Trade 1823.

Appendix B

Headquarters buildings occupied by the Board of Trade

'To the south of the Treasury Passage, the premises fronting the street ... in 1768 the Board of Trade was established here.'

1782   Board of Trade abolished

1786   Board of Trade reconstituted in the same building

1824   Soane plans for a facade from Downing Street to the Treasury Passage (Treasury Passage closed 1826)

1827   Soane facade complete

1844   Barry plans for 'New Treasury Offices'

1845   Soane facade dismantled

1846   'New Treasury Offices' complete; frontage from Downing Street to Dover House

1872–73   Move of Board of Trade to Whitehall Gardens

1920   Great George Street

1940   Millbank (ICI House)

1952   Horse Guards Avenue

1963–64   Move of Board of Trade to 1 Victoria Street

178. Soane's new facade of the Board of Trade and Privy Council Offices, 1828.

Appendix C

Chronology

Including principal organisational changes, selected legislation and published reports.

1621   Committee of the Privy Council for Trade and Plantations established.

1660   Two Councils appointed: one to look after the plantations, the other for trade.

1696   Permanent Committee – the Board of Trade and Plantations – established by William III.

1780   Edmund Burke's speech urging abolition of the Board of Trade.

1782   Civil List & Secret Service Money Act 1782 abolished the Board of Trade.

1784   Order in Council reconstituted the Board as a Committee of the Privy Council for 'consideration of all matters relating to trade and foreign plantations'.

1786   Order in Council appointed a new Committee of the Privy Council. From this Order the Board of Trade developed, its secretariat was strengthened and took on a permanent shape.

1825   Consolidation of existing revenue laws carried out by William Huskisson, when President.

1828   Board of Trade assumed control over Comptroller of Corn Returns.

1830   Opening of Manchester-Liverpool Railway, and accidental death of Huskisson.

1832   Board of Trade Statistical department set up.

1837   First government school of industrial design opened, at Somerset House.

1839   Designs Registry opened.

1840   Railway department created within Board of Trade.

1842   Second major revision of the tariff.

1845   Third major revision of the tariff.

1846   Railway functions transferred to an independent Board of Railway Commissioners.

1848   Initiative in tariff matters transferred to Treasury from Board of Trade, following replacement of protective tariff by a tariff for revenue.

1850   Mercantile Marine Act 1850 constituted the Board of Trade as the authority to 'undertake the general superintendence of matters relating to the British mercantile marine'.

1851   Board of Trade's railway responsibilities returned, and Railway Commissioners abolished.
Great Exhibition

1852   Museum of Ornamental Art (origin of V & A Museum) set up under the Board of Trade.

1853   Science division established under the Department of Science & Art of the Board of Trade (origin of Science Museum).

1854   Canals became the responsibility of the Board.
Merchant Shipping Act 1854 consolidated all previous marine legislation.

1855   Meteorological department established, headed by Captain Fitzroy 'for the discussion of meteorological observations made at sea in all parts of the globe'.
Certain duties concerning registry of British merchant ships were transferred to Board of Trade from Board of Customs.

1856	New Department of Education took over Science & Art Department.
1860	Cobden Treaty with France, on tariffs and free trade.
1861	Harbours and Passing Tolls, etc, Act. Section 65 of this act lays down for the first time that 'The Lords of the Committee of Privy Council appointed for the Consideration of Matters relating to Trade and Foreign Plantations may be described in all Acts of Parliament, Deeds, Contracts, and other instruments, by the official Title of "the Board of Trade" without expressing their names...'

1864	Select Committee appointed to 'inquire into the arrangement between the Foreign Office and the Board of Trade with reference to the trade with foreign nations'.
1866	Under the Standards Act 1866 custody of the standards, weights and measures, transferred to Board of Trade.
1867	Control of foreshores and certain fisheries powers, were transferred to the Board of Trade.
	Abolition of office of Vice-President of the Board of Trade, and institution of a Secretary, having a seat in Parliament.
	Admiralty passed to Board of Trade,

179. The new public offices at Whitehall. Sir Charles Barry's re-design of Soane's facade at the Board of Trade, 1846.

	general navigation jurisdiction over lighthouses, pilotage, wrecks and foreshore rights.
1872	Consultative business of the Board's Commercial department and the commercial library, were transferred to the Foreign Office. The Board's Statistical department was united with the old Commercial department.
1875	Trade Marks Act.
1876	Trade Marks Registry founded.
1877	Solicitor's department formed.
1879	Tay Bridge disaster.
1882	Commercial treaty work returned to Board from Foreign Office.
1883	Bankruptcy Act 1883 transferred administration of the bankruptcy acts from the Courts to the Board of Trade, and a Bankruptcy department was set up within the Board.
	Patent Act 1883, under which the granting of patents was assigned to a Comptroller-General of patents, designs and trade marks, under control of the Board of Trade.
1886	*Board of Trade Journal* first published.
	Board of Trade began to collect labour statistics.
	Fisheries department for England & Wales set up in the Board of Trade.
1888	Railway & Canal Commission set up, and powers of control over the administration of railways and canals conferred on the Board.
1892	Corn returns work went to the new Board of Agriculture.
1893	Labour department created within the Board, and *Labour Gazette* first appeared.
	Hubert Llewellyn Smith appointed as first Labour Commissioner.
1896	Conciliation Act 1896 gave Board authority to negotiate in trade disputes.
1899	Commercial Intelligence branch set up within Board.

1900	National Physical Laboratory set up with a Board of Trade member of its Executive Council.
1902	National Physical Laboratory opened.
1903	Fisheries work transferred to Board of Agriculture.
1903	Imperial Institute managed by Board of Trade.
1906	Census of Production Act.
1907	Patents & Designs Act.
1908	First Trade Commissioner posts established in four Dominions.
	Board of Trade empowered to set up a Court of Arbitration in industrial disputes.
	Port of London Authority set up, and controlled by Board of Trade.
1909	Trade Boards Act provided for establishment by the Board of Trade of trade boards (later renamed Wages Councils) principally to fix minimum rates of pay in certain trades.
1909/10	Network of labour exchanges set up under Labour Exchanges Act 1909.
1911	Commercial & Statistical department of Board separated from Labour department.
	National Insurance Act.
	Copyright Act.
	Department of the Government Chemist set up under Treasury control.
1912	Wreck of the *Titanic*.
1913	Unemployment insurance administered by the Board of Trade through labour exchanges. Separate department set up in the Board under an Assistant Secretary for labour exchanges and unemployment insurance work; the Board's department of Labour Statistics put under a director.
1914	War declared, 4 August.
	Custodianship of enemy property passed from Board to Public Trustee.
	War Trade Department set up to deal with export licensing.
	Maintenance of harbours transferred to

1915 Board of Agriculture & Fisheries.
Ministry of Munitions set up.

1916 Ministry of Shipping took over sea transport and ship construction.
Petrol Control department added to Board of Trade.
Management of Imperial Institute transferred to Colonial Office.
Department of Scientific & Industrial Research set up.

1917 Department of Overseas Trade, jointly responsible to Foreign Office and Board of Trade, formed.
Ministry of Reconstruction created.
Ministry of Labour took over labour responsibilities, department of Labour Statistics, labour exchanges and unemployment insurance work from the Board of Trade.

Royal Commission on Dominions Trade.
Coalfields taken over, and production, pricing and distribution of coal, management and development of collieries and employment of miners subject to the direction of a Coal Controller working through a Mines department within the Board of Trade.

1918 Industries & Manufactures department of Board of Trade established.
Armistice Day, 11 November.

1919 Railway responsibilities, canals, electricity supply and Marine department were taken over by the Ministry of Transport. Board's Harbour department was wound up. The Board retained its duties in connection with lighthouses, pilotage, and related matters. War Trade Department was taken over by Board.

180. Board of Trade, 1852.

Export Credits department (forerunner of ECGD) set up as part of the Department of Overseas Trade.

Accidents Investigation Branch formed, to become part of Air Ministry in 1922.

Ministry of Reconstruction abolished.

Chief Economic Adviser appointed in Board of Trade.

Board of Electricity Commissioners set up for 'promoting, regulating and supervising the supply of electricity'.

1920 Under Mining Industry Act 1920, the Mines department of the Board of Trade was set up under a Parliamentary Secretary of the Board, but remained autonomous.

Certain powers relating to company and private water undertakings were transferred to the Ministry of Health.

Certain powers relating to electricity were transferred to the Ministry of Transport.

Board of Trade took over some powers and duties relating to local authority gas undertakings.

1921 Marine department returned to Board of Trade; renamed Mercantile Marine department.

Transport department of the Admiralty transferred to Board of Trade.

Ministry of Food dissolved, and its residual functions moved mainly to Board of Trade.

1922 Control of registration of business names went to Board of Trade.

Certain powers concerning railway and canal traffic and the Port of London were transferred to Ministry of Transport.

1923 Board of Trade assumed responsibility for the Coastguard service.

Registration of business names transferred to Board of Inland Revenue (which was already responsible for registration of companies).

1925 Board of Trade took over Custodian of Enemy Property work for England & Wales from Public Trustee.

Responsibility for the Imperial Institute given to Department of Overseas Trade.

1928 Functions relating to petroleum were passed to Mines department.

1930 Export Credits Guarantee Department became independent, with its own Vote.

1932 Import Duties Act. Independent Import Duties Advisory Committee appointed; its recommendations were reviewed by the Board of Trade.

1936 Food (defence plans) department established within Board of Trade.

1939 War declared, 3 September.

Regulations under Emergency Powers (Defence) Act gave Board of Trade powers to regulate or prohibit production, storage, distribution or consumption, to license business transactions, control prices and introduce and operate control schemes.

Food department given independent status as wartime Ministry of Food.

Ministry of Supply created.

New Ministry of Shipping took over Board's shipping work.

Import Duties Advisory Committee dissolved, and duties transferred to Board of Trade.

Petroleum powers transferred to Ministry of Supply

Public Trustee appointed Custodian of Enemy Property for England & Wales, by Board of Trade.

1940 Export Council set up.

Petroleum department created, under a Parliamentary Secretary of the Board of Trade.

Royal Commission on the Distribution of the Industrial Population, Report. HMSO, 1940, reprinted 1967. Cmd 6153. (Chairman: Sir M Barlow)

1941 Clothes rationing introduced.

Board of Trade made responsible for war damage claims for chattels.

1942 Utility Furniture Scheme announced.

Ministry of Fuel & Power established, with duties taken from Board of Trade relating to coal, gas, electricity, petroleum, mines and quarries. Board of Trade Petroleum department and Mines department abolished.

Ministry of Production set up as co-ordinating authority linking the three main supply departments: Admiralty, Supply and Aircraft Production.

Trading with the Enemy Department set up by Treasury and Board of Trade.

1944 Council of Industrial Design founded. Ministry of Reconstruction. *Employment Policy*. HMSO, 1944, Cmd 6527.

1945 Post of Minister of Reconstruction abolished.

In May posts of President of the Board of Trade and Minister of Production held by one man. Ministry of Production merged into Board of Trade later that year.

Distribution of Industry Act gave Board of Trade general responsibility for distribution of industry and development area policy. This had formerly been part of the functions of the Ministry of Labour & National Service.

1946 Department of Overseas Trade abolished and its functions returned to a new Export Promotions division within the Board of Trade. Post of Secretary for Overseas Trade was retained.

Control of all raw materials except iron and steel, non-ferrous and light metals was transferred to Board of Trade from Ministry of Supply.

1947 General Agreement on Tariffs and Trade signed.

181. Whitehall Gardens, 1914.

Regional boards for industry transferred to newly appointed Minister for Economic Affairs; later that year the Ministry for Economic Affairs was absorbed into the Treasury.

National Engineering Laboratory established.

Statistics of Trade Act.

1948   Companies Act. Companies registration was transferred to Board of Trade from Board of Inland Revenue.

Monopolies & Restrictive Practices (enquiry and control) Act, under which the Monopolies (now Monopolies & Mergers) Commission was set up.

National Research & Development Corporation founded.

Duties of Custodian of Enemy Property returned to Board of Trade.

1949   Responsibility for Imperial Institute passed to Ministry of Education.

1950   Control over labelling of food containers transferred to Board from Ministry of Food.

1951   Ministry of Materials established, with functions transferred from Board of Trade and Ministry of Supply. Responsible for raw materials up to time when they entered manufacturing industry.

1952   Regional boards for industry returned to Board from Treasury.

1953   Post of Secretary for Overseas Trade abolished; his duties relating to ECGD transferred to President of the Board of Trade.

Board of Trade to co-ordinate work of Departments in connection with industrial productivity.

1954   Ministry of Materials dissolved and its work given to Board.

1955   Ministry of Supply transferred to Board of Trade responsibility for iron and steel and non-ferrous metals industries, and engineering industry.

1956   Registrar of Restrictive Trading Agreements appointed at Board of Trade.
Copyright Act.

1957   Board of Trade transferred, to Minister of Power, functions relating to iron and steel.

1958   Import Duties Act.
First sitting of Restrictive Practices Court.
ECGD made responsible directly to President of the Board of Trade.

1959   Warren Spring Laboratory established.

1960   European Free Trade Association Convention signed.
Three industrial estates management corporations set up to manage Board of Trade industrial property.

1962   *Committee on Consumer Protection, Final report.* HMSO, 1962, Cmnd 1781. (Chairman: J T Molony)

1963   Location of Offices Bureau established.
New post of Secretary of State for Industry, Trade and Regional Development created, and held jointly with Presidency of Board of Trade.

1964   Control of merchant shipping returned to Board of Trade.
Regional policy transferred to new Department of Economic Affairs.

1965   Queen's Award to Industry Scheme launched.

1966   Board of Trade given responsibility for civil aviation.

1967   *Final report of the Court of Inquiry into certain matters concerning the Shipping Industry.* HMSO, 1967, Cmnd 3211. (Chairman: Rt Hon Lord Pearson)

1969   Business Statistics Office moved to Newport, Gwent.
Ministry of Power absorbed into Ministry of Technology.
Committee of Inquiry into Civil Air Transport. *British air transport in the seventies. Report.* HMSO, 1969, Cmnd 4018. (Chairman: Sir Ronald Edwards)

1970 Computer Aided Design Centre established.
Department of Trade and Industry came into being, uniting the Board of Trade and the Ministry of Technology. New Secretary of State retained office of President of the Board of Trade.
Committee of Inquiry into Shipping, Report. HMSO, 1970, Cmnd 4337. (Chairman: The Rt Hon the Viscount Rochdale)

1971 Civil Aviation Authority created.
DTI took over responsibility for the aerospace industry, Concorde and Rolls Royce.
Commission on the Third London Airport, Report. HMSO, 1971, (Chairman: The Hon Mr Justice Roskill)
Consumer Credit, Report of the Committee. HMSO, 1971, Cmnd 4596. (Chairman: Lord Crowther)
Committee of Inquiry on Small Firms, Report. HMSO, 1971. Cmnd 4811. (Chairman: J E Bolton)
Report of the Advisory Group on Shipbuilding on the Upper Clyde ... dated July 29 1971. HMSO 1971, HC 544.

1972 British Overseas Trade Board established.
Report of the Tribunal appointed to inquire into certain issues in relation to the circumstances leading up to the cessation of trading by the Vehicle and General Insurance Company Limited. HMSO, 1972, HL 80, HC 133.

1973 UK became a member of the European Community
Office of Fair Trading established under the Fair Trading Act 1973.
Price Commission established under the Counter-Inflation Act 1973.

1974 DTI split up to form three new departments: Department of Trade, Department of Industry, and Department of Prices and Consumer Protection.
Department of Energy formed from energy divisions within DTI.

Ministry of Posts & Telecommunications dissolved and its work incorporated into new Department of Industry.

1976 National Enterprise Board founded.
Copyright and Designs Law. Report of the Committee to consider the law on copyright and designs. HMSO, 1977, Cmnd 6732. (Chairman: The Hon Mr Justice Whitford)

1979 Following General Election, Department of Prices & Consumer Protection abolished, and its responsibilities transferred to Department of Trade.

1981 National Enterprise Board merged with National Research & Development Corporation to form the British Technology Group.

1982 National Maritime Institute privatised.

1983 Departments of Trade and of Industry merged to form new DTI.
Radio Regulatory division transferred from Home Office to DTI.
Responsibility for civil aviation and shipping transferred to Department of Transport.
Computer Aided Design Centre privatised.

1984 DTI *Aims* published
Oftel (Office of Telecommunications) set up.
British Telecom privatised.

1985 Insolvency Act.
Films Act.
Companies Act.
Responsibility for small firms and tourism transferred to Department of Employment.

Appendix D

Bibliography

This bibliography is a list of sources consulted, and is not intended as a comprehensive set of references to the Board of Trade, although including the major sources on the subject. It is arranged in two sequences: the first of general material, the second of items specifically concerned with my subject. A number of Command papers will be found in the Chronology.

General: books and articles

ASPINALL, A AND SMITH, E A. English historical documents 1783-1832. Eyre & Spottiswoode, 1959. *XI*

BEVERIDGE, J. Beveridge and his plan. Hodder & Stoughton, 1954.

BIGNELL, P. Taking the train: railway travel in Victorian times. National Railway Museum/Science Museum. HMSO, 1978.

BOOTH, A. 'The second world war and the origins of modern regional policy.' *Economy and Society, XI* (1) 1982, pp 1-21.

BRITISH RAIL. *London Midland Region.* Rocket 150: 150th anniversary of the Liverpool & Manchester Railway 1830-1980. Official handbook. British Rail, 1980.

BROCKWAY, T P. Rationing in Britain 1939—1945. 1950 [Unpublished preliminary draft of the third volume of a series of studies of rationing during World War Two, undertaken by Harvard University]

BURK, K. *ed.* War and the state: the transformation of British government 1914-19. Allen & Unwin, 1982.

BURKE, E. Speech of Edmund Burke Esq, Member of Parliament for the city of Bristol, on presenting to the House of Commons (on the 11th of February. 1780): A plan for the better security of the independence of Parliament, and the economical reformation of the civil and other establishment. A new edition. Printed for J Dodsley, in Pall-Mall, 1780.

CENTRAL OFFICE OF INFORMATION. *Reference division. Home Front Section.* Rationing and distribution schemes in Great Britain. COI, 1944.

CHANDOS, Oliver Lyttelton. 1st *Viscount.* The memoirs of Lord Chandos. The Bodley Head, 1962.

CHECKLAND, S. British public policy 1776-1939: an economic, social and political perspective. Cambridge University Press, 1983.

DAILY TELEGRAPH. 125 years in words and pictures, as described in contemporary reports in the *Daily Telegraph* 1855-1980. n.d. [1980]

DALTON, H. The fateful years: memoirs 1931-1945. Muller, 1957.

DUGDALE, G S. Whitehall through the centuries. Phoenix House Ltd, 1950.

GREYSMITH, D 'Patterns, piracy and protection in the textile printing industry 1787-1850.' *Textile History 14* (2), 1983, pp 165-194.

HARGREAVES, E L AND GOWING, M M. Civil industry and trade. HMSO and Longmans Green & Co, 1952. (History of the Second World War)

A history of ECGD 1919/1979. ECGD, 1979.

JAMES, R.R. Churchill: a study in failure 1909-1939. Weidenfeld & Nicolson, 1970.

LAMBERT, A J. Nineteenth century railway history through the *Illustrated London News.* David & Charles, 1984.

LEE, C E. The Metropolitan Line: a brief history. London Transport, 1972.

LOWE, R. 'The erosion of state intervention in Britain 1917—1924.' *Economic History Review,* 2nd series *XXXI* (2). February 1978, pp 270—286.

MCKECHNIE, S. The romance of the civil service. Sampson Low, Marston & Co Ltd [1930]

MARSH, E. A number of people: a book of reminiscences. Heinemann in association with Hamish Hamilton, 1939.

MORGAN, K O ed. The Oxford illustrated history of Britain. Oxford University Press, 1984.

NATIONAL ENGINEERING LABORATORY. Introducing NEL. 1981

'NMI Ltd — A new era'. *NMI News*. A special edition October 1982 [8] pp.

150 years of the Liverpool & Manchester Railway: pictures, books and commemorative ceramics drawn from the Elton Collection. Catalogue of exhibition at the Coach House Gallery, Darby Road, Coalbrookdale, 7 June to 30 November, 1980.

PIKE, E. R. Human documents of the industrial revolution in Britain. Allen & Unwin, 1966.

PIKE, E R. Human documents of the Lloyd George era. Allen & Unwin, 1972.

PYATT, E. The National Physical Laboratory: a history. Adam Hilger Ltd, 1983.

RANDALL, P. 'The history of British regional policy.' *In* Regional policy for ever? Essays on the history, theory and political economy of forty years of 'regionalism'. Institute of Economic Affairs, 1973, pp 17-58.

SHANNON, H A. 'The coming of general limited liability.' *Economic History II*, January 1931, pp 267-291.

STAMP, G. The changing metropolis. Viking, 1984.

THOMPSON, C R compiler. The first 60 years. The story of the development of the Schermuly Pistol Rocket Apparatus Ltd, issued on the occasion of its Diamond Jubilee 1897-1957. n.d. [1957]

TREASURY. *Organisation & methods division.* Historical table of changes in government organisation. 1957.

TWENTIETH CENTURY. Drawn and quartered. The world of the British newspaper cartoon. Times Newspapers Ltd for the Newspaper Publishers Association, n.d. [1970]

VERNON, R AND MANSERGH, N eds. Advisory bodies: a study of their uses in relation to central government 1919—1939. Allen & Unwin, 1940.

WALKER, M Daily sketches. A cartoon history of twentieth century Britain. Muller, 1978.

WALPOLE, K A 'The humanitarian movement of the early nineteenth century to remedy abuses on emigrant vessels to America.' *Transactions of the Royal Historical Society XIV* 1931, pp 197-224.

WARREN SPRING LABORATORY. Environmental and industrial process technology 1959-1984 [1984]

WHITESIDE, N 'Welfare insurance and casual labour: a study of administrative intervention in industrial employment, 1906-26.' *Economic History Review,* 2nd series *XXXII* (4) November 1979, pp 507-522.

WILLSON, F M G, ed CHESTER, D N. The organisation of British central government 1914-1964: a survey by a study group of the Royal Institute of Public Administration. 2nd ed. Allen & Unwin, 1968.

YOUNG, G M and HANDCOCK, W D eds. English historical documents, 1833-1874. Eyre & Spottiswoode, 1956. *XII* (I)

Books and articles on the Board of Trade

BADHAM, C. The life of James Deacon Hume, Secretary of the Board of Trade. Smith, Elder & Co, 1859.

BASYE, A H. The Lords Commissioners of Trade and Plantations, commonly known as the Board of Trade 1748-1782. Yale University Press/Oxford University Press, 1925.

BENNETT, J AND CANNONS, M compilers, ed STOREY, R. The first Labour correspondent and the Board of Trade Library. University of Warwick Library, 1984. (Occasional publications no II)

BLAKE, *Sir* J. 'The centenary of the Patent Office.' *Nature* (170) 1952, pp 1044-1046.

'Board of Trade and Plantations'. *Pinnock's Guide to Knowledge* no CXXXVII, 4 October 1834, [2] pp.

BOARD OF TRADE. Cost of living of the working classes. Report of an enquiry by the Board of Trade into working-class rents and retail prices, together with the rates of wages in certain occupations in industrial towns of the United Kingdom in 1912 (in continuation of a similar enquiry in 1905). HMSO, 1913, Cd 6955.

BOARD OF TRADE. An introduction to the Board of Trade. 1969.

The Board of Trade, its origin, authority and jurisdiction, orginally prepared by Mr Roscoe and revised by Mr Farrer. Board of Trade, 1880.

The Board of Trade: its origin, authority and jurisdiction [1914]

BOARD OF TRADE. List of Board of Trade records to 1913. New York. Kraus Reprint Corporation, 1964.

BOARD OF TRADE. List of public records retained in the Board of Trade, 1846–1885. [1936]

BOARD OF TRADE. Memorandum with respect to the re-organisation of the Board of trade. HMSO, 1918. Cd 8912.

BOARD OF TRADE. Report on the Board of Trade, by Sir E Tennent. 1862.

BOARD OF TRADE. Report on the Board of Trade [dated the 27th November 1866] by S Cave and G Ward Hunt. 1866.

'The Board of Trade [1905–1907]' In Davies, W.W. Lloyd George 1863–1914. Constable, 1939, pp 238–281.

Boneblack. Board of Trade staff magazine. I (1–4), February 1924–March 1925.

British business, formerly Trade and Industry [1970–1979], previously Board of Trade Journal [1886–1970]

BROWN, L. The Board of Trade and the free-trade movement 1830–42. Clarendon Press, 1958.

CLARKE, M P. 'The Board of Trade at work.' American Historical Review, XVII, 1912, pp 17–43.

COMMITTEE FOR TRADE AND PLANTATIONS. Study of the slave trade. 28 March 1789. Presented to the House by William Pitt, 25 April 1789.

COSGRAVE, P. 'Government, business and the monster of the DTI.' Spectator, 30 June 1973, p 807.

CRAIG, Sir J. A history of red tape: an account of the origin and development of the civil service. Macdonald & Evans Ltd, 1955.

CYRIAX, G 'The Board of Trade,' New Society, 24 October 1963, pp 14—15.

DAVIDSON, R. 'The Board of Trade and industrial relations 1896—1914.' Historical Journal, 21 (3) 1978, pp 571–591.

DAVIDSON, R. 'Llewellyn Smith, the Labour Department and government growth 1886–1909.' In Sutherland, G ed. Studies in the growth of nineteenth century government. Routledge & Kegan Paul, 1972. pp 227–262

DEPARTMENT OF TRADE AND INDUSTRY. Aims. January 1984.

'The Department goes to war.' Tie-line: staff newspaper of the Departments of Trade and Industry, June 1982, no 115, p1.

DEPARTMENT OF TRADE. National Weights and Measures Laboratory. 1981.

EASTERFIELD, T E. 'The Special Research Unit at the Board of Trade. 1946–1949.' Journal of Operational Research, 34 (7) 1983, pp 565–568.

FROST J. The naughty Board of Trade: a hundred and thirty years of government regulation of British merchant shipping. n.d. [1978?] Unpublished.

HARDING, H. Patent Office centenary: a story of 100 years in the life and work of the Patent Office. HMSO, 1953.

HOLROYD, J E. 'Seventy five years of the Board of Trade Journal.' Board of Trade Journal, 15 September 1961, pp 549–554.

HOLROYD, J E. 'Eighty four years of the Board of Trade Journal.' Trade and Industry, 21 October 1970, pp 7–8

HORN, D B. 'The Board of Trade and consular reports 1696–1782.' English Historical Review 54, 1939, pp 476–480.

HOWELL, D. 'Decline and fall.' Spectator, 2 May 1970, pp 578–9.

HYDE, F E. Mr Gladstone at the Board of Trade. Cobden-Sanderson, 1934.

INTERDEPARTMENTAL COMMITTEE ON SOCIAL & ECONOMIC RESEARCH. Census of Production reports. HMSO, 1961 (Guides to official sources: no 6)

KELF-COHEN, R. 'The Board of Trade fifty years ago.' The Times, 19 March 1964, p 13.

KIRBY, M W. 'The politics of state coercion in inter-war Britain: the Mines Department of the Board of Trade, 1920–1942.' Historical Journal, 2 (2) 1979, pp 373–396.

Labour Gazette 1, May-December 1893.

LEE, Sir F. The Board of Trade. Athlone Press, 1958 (The Stamp Memorial Lecture 1958)

LINGELBACH, A L. 'The inception of the British Board of Trade.' *American Historical Review XXX* (4) July 1925, pp 701-727.

LINGELBACH, A L. 'William Huskisson as President of the Board of Trade.' *American Historical Review XLIII* (4) July 1938, pp 759-774.

LLEWELLYN SMITH, *Sir* H. The Board of Trade. G P Putnam's Sons Ltd, 1928.

MILLER, H. 'The Board of Trade.' *Vickers Magazine,* Winter 1965-66, pp 17-22.

PARKHURST, P G. Ships of peace: a record of some of the problems which came before the Board of Trade in connection with the British mercantile marine from early days to the year 1885. 1962.

THE PATENT OFFICE, DEPARTMENT OF TRADE. A century of trade marks: a commentary on the work and history of the Trade Marks Registry, which celebrates its centenary in 1976. HMSO, 1976.

THE PATENT OFFICE. An introduction to the services of the Patent Office and the Trade Marks and Design Registries, prepared for the Department of Trade and Industry by the Central Office of Information. HMSO, 1983.

PROUTY, R. The transformation of the Board of Trade 1830-1855: a study of administrative reorganization in the heyday of laissez-faire. Heinemann, 1957.

PUBLIC RECORD OFFICE. Index to Board of Trade papers, 1846-1865, deposited in the Public Record Office. 1900.

The Queen's Award to Industry. Report of the 1975 review committee. HMSO, 1975.

Report of a Committee appointed to consider certain questions relating to the Meteorological Department of the Board of Trade. Eyre & Spottiswoode, for HMSO, 1866.

Report of a formal investigation into the circumstances attending the foundering on 15th April 1912, of the British steamship 'Titanic' ... HMSO, 1912. Cd 6352.

SAINTY, J C. Officials of the Boards of trade 1660-1870. Athlone Press, 1974.

Tie-line: staff newspaper of the Departments of Trade and Industry (Oct 1972—Feb 1985; later *DTI News* (March 1985 —   )

WILDE, J H. 'The creation of the Marine Department of the Board of Trade.' *Journal of Transport History II* (4), November 1956, pp 193-206.

WOODS, *Sir* J H. 'Administrative problems of the Board of Trade.' *Public Administration 26* (2) 1948, pp 85-91.

182. The Board of Trade, from Parliament Square by Frank L Emanuel.

Past and then existent members of the Staff of the Finance Department, Board of Trade, summer of 1910.
Names counting position, left to right

(Standing) 1. Charles Jones† 2. W.D. Russell (Bank† Dept) 3. J. Tandon (Labour Dept) 4. C.H. Gann 5. G. Norman 6. H.B. Smith 7. W. Greig 8. N. Stanger (Bank† Dept) 9. C. Thandon (Companies Dept) 10. C.A.A. Wolff, 11. J.W. Cornish 12. W.F. Stone (Ministry of Labour) 13. J.W. Fletcher 14. Wm. Smith 15 A.L.W. Gay 16. F.J. Legg 17. J.E. Nicholls 18 E. Fowler (Ministry of Labour) 19. T.W.F. Dalton (Ministry of Labour) 20. R. Geal (Bankruptcy Dept) 21. B.C. Page 22. D. Callingham 23 F.J. Littleton 24. W.S. Hood 25. J.H. Dallas 26 A.L. Mackie (Ministry of Labour) 27. E. Lucas 28. Arthur Mills (Bankruptcy) 29. H.A. Bamford 30. J. Le Bondall 31. E.A. Wilberton 32. F.W. Emler 33. S. Nimberson (Stationery Off) 34. P.H. Russell

(Sitting) 1. A.S. Lake 2. H.C. Watson (Bankruptcy - retired 1918) 3. G.B. Shephard 4. C. Wright (Companies) 5. A. Barnes VSO 6. J. Goldie (retired) 7. S.S. Fay CBE 8. R. Brown (retired) 9. F.C. Stoneham O.B.E. 10. H. Townsend, 11. R.J. Sheldon 12. G.W. Isons

† those so indicated died prior to 1919

Photograph taken in garden at rear of 7 Whitehall Gardens, the eighteenth century residence of the Earls of Pembroke.

183. Past and then existent members of the staff of the Finance department, Board of Trade, Summer, 1910.

144

Index

For the Board of Trade see under 'Board'. Entries for all other Departments are inverted (eg Energy, Department of). Numbers in *italic* refer to pictures. Names of ships, trains, films and publications are in italic.

BACK COVER: Whitehall in 1823, by F Nugent. The Board of Trade is centre left. St Martins-in-the-Fields can be seen above the houses.